CLOSER TO HEAVEN

Also by Don Maclean
FLYING HIGH

CLOSER TO HEAVEN

Don Maclean

248

Hodder & Stoughton

LONDON   SYDNEY   AUCKLAND

Copyright © 2004 by Don Maclean and Chris Gidney

First published in Great Britain in 2004

The right of Don Maclean and Chris Gidney to be identified as
the Authors of the Work has been asserted by them in accordance
with the Copyright, Designs and Patents Act 1988.

10 9 8 7 6 5 4 3 2 1

British Library Cataloguing in Publication Data
A record for this book is available from the British Library

ISBN 0 340 78690 6

Printed and bound in Great Britain by Clays Ltd,
St Ives plc, Bungay, Suffolk

The paper used in this book is a natural recyclable product
made from wood grown in sustainable forests.
The hard coverboard is recycled.

Hodder & Stoughton
A Division of Hodder Headline Ltd
338 Euston Road
London NW1 3BH
www.madaboutbooks.com

Contents

Foreword   xi
Acknowledgements   xiv
Introduction   xv

CHURCH

Sunday Best   1
Suffer from Little Children   4
Excuses   6
God's Painter   8

PRAYER

Go on – Ask   10
Not Yet   12
Only the Best   15
Help Me Pray, Lord   16
Prayer for Our World   17
Out of My Control   18

CLOSER TO HEAVEN

Eugene   20
Growin' Old   23
Resignation   25
God on the Line   28
ASAP   33

PEOPLE

Heroes   34
Jozy Pollock   38
Sex Symbol   40
Heart of the Matter   42
Biodots   45
Mind the Trap   48

MONEY

Filthy Lucre   50
Money Isn't Everything   52
Let's Play   53
All the Rage   55
Putting Problems into Perspective   57

CONTENTS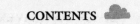

LIFE AND DEATH

It's a Gift	58
Grandma's Stocking	59
Whatever Life Throws at Me	61
Life Explained	62
Bow and Exit Left	65
What Fore?	66
Journey's End	69
Struggles	71
Numbers Up	73
9/11	76

CHRISTMAS AND EASTER

'Twas the Night Before Christmas	78
Bethlehem	85
Good Friday	86
Good Friday Prayer	90
Easter Day!	91
Easter People's Prayer	95

GOD'S CHARACTER

All Around	97
You're a Pea Hans	99
Never Alone	102
Technical Support	104
God's Job	109
Rugby Speaks Louder than Words	111
Satan's Menu	113
Trying to Connect You	115
Hotel Bibles	119
God's Positive Answers	120
Lead Us, Heavenly Father, Lead Us	123
God's Pitch	125
A Perfect Altar	128
Born Again	130

FAITH

Are You Sitting Comfortably?	132
Use Your Muscles	134
How to See God	136
The Bright Side	139
Keep Calm	141

CONTENTS

What Prints?   143
Shining Brightly   144

CHILDREN AND FAMILIES

Our Fathers   145
Fathers' Prayer   147
Fishes and Men   148
Single Parents Find It Tough   152
Daughters   154
From the Mouths of Babes   157
What Really Counts   159
Keep Looking Up   161
Birds and Bees   163

BIBLE

The Earth Project   165
Psalm Twenty-three-and-a-half   168
Instructions Included   170
Lessons from Noah   172
The Lost Chapter of Genesis   173
Interviews I Wish I'd Done No. 1   177

CLOSER TO HEAVEN

Interviews I Wish I'd Done No. 2   181
Can God Really Use Me?   185
Bible Hit Parade   187
The Bible in Fifty Words   191

Foreword

DON MACLEAN, star of numerous television and stage shows, is certainly a high-flyer. Not just because he has been the presenter of Radio 2's most listened-to Sunday morning programme for more than thirteen years and gets to travel around the world, but because he actually flies his own plane. I know, because I've seen it close up.

When I met Don's plane, a Piper Tomahawk, and asked him to open the bonnet I couldn't believe my eyes. Peering inside, to me, a neophyte, it looked so small and insignificant.

'My lawnmower engine is bigger than that!' I yelped. 'However can such a tiny engine get all this heavy metal and two people off the ground?' I asked incredulously.

'Simple,' came Don's reply. 'Faith.'

What he meant was that fuel, aerodynamics and the skill of a pilot when combined with the tiny electrical spark can create enough energy to lift a very heavy load skyward.

Now Don has a Grumman Tiger with the registration G-DONI, a four-seater with a powerful engine, but the lesson remains the same. We all need the elements of divine fuel, a spiritual framework surrounding us, and God as our pilot to get us through life to heaven beyond. However, the tiny spark that sets it all off must come from within.

Despite feeling closer to heaven when in the clouds, Don is really a man with both feet solidly placed on terra firma. Every time he encounters turbulence in the skies, he is reminded that the everyday ups and downs of life on earth bring struggles that are sometimes hard to manage alone.

For Don, the key to whatever life presents has always been his Christian faith and *Closer to Heaven* is Don's answer to the mystery of life, its fears, loneliness and struggle. Based on his experiences as a family man, international entertainer and broadcaster, *Closer to Heaven* is packed with stimulating thoughts to ignite a spiritual spark within every reader, alongside a few laughs.

Presented in an easy-to-read format, *Closer to Heaven* features Don's favourite hymns, Bible verses, poems and quotes, personal words of wisdom and prayers written by Don to bring hope, comfort and inspiration. Drawn from his immense experience of meeting the most famous and infamous people the world has to offer, it offers an abundance of thoughtful, bite-sized and contemporary reading to stimulate and encourage.

Closer to Heaven follows Don's highly successful autobiography, Flying High, and celebrates what has inspired him in the worldwide Church as it draws the reader to look closer to heaven for motivation and guidance in a difficult and confusing world.

CHRIS GIDNEY, 2004

Acknowledgements

I AM GRATEFUL to all those who have sent me stories, poems and prayers over the years, some of which I have been able to include here. Many stories are new to me but perhaps have been around for a long time and become like 'Chinese Whispers'.

I have credited those where I can, but if there are any included here that should be credited to someone unknown to me, please let me know so that I can correct this in any future imprint of this edition.

Thanks to Chris Gidney – my editor and book encourager; Judith Longman at Hodder & Stoughton; and special thanks to my wife, Toni; daughter, Rachel; son, Rory; and granddaughters, Gracie and Francesca; all of whom have provided experiential material for this book!

Finally my thanks to God who sticks with me whether he finds me in tears or laughter and often both!

Introduction

WELCOME to my book …

When I began to write it, I had great hopes of a philosophical work, outlining my beliefs, theories and observations on life. I read the first chapter; it was ever so pompous. It sounded like *The Thoughts of Chairman Don*, not the sort of thing you'd want to read at all. 'Think again, Don,' I told myself. So I thought of little things that had happened to me, little thoughts that had passed through my mind and in so doing had confirmed the presence of God in my life. Listeners constantly send me their thoughts too, together with poems, sayings and snippets of wisdom. I've kept some of them over the years and thought I'd include them as well in this melange. You may find it more like a blancmange, but I hope it's more of a heavenly take-away, something you can dip into as and when you feel spiritually peckish. Hopefully you'll find all manner of divine morsels: a good read, plenty of laughs, some spicy bits, a real challenge, a dash of comfort and a big helping of inspiration. I hope you'll feel you've had a good snack to fill the gap whenever you take a peek inside.

CHURCH

Sunday Best

CLEANLINESS IS next to godliness but only if several pages are missing from your dictionary. Mom and I always got dressed up on a Sunday morning for our trip to nine o'clock mass at the church of St John the Evangelist; so did everyone else. The ladies all wore hats in those days or perhaps mantillas, which gave them a mysterious, Spanish look. My hair was plastered down with Dad's Brylcreem and my shoes shone. I was always upset if it was a rainy day and the toes of my shoes and the backs of my socks were spattered in mud. I'm no longer quite so bothered about my appearance on Sunday mornings. Let's be honest, most people tend to turn up as though they've put on the first thing that came to hand; there's no such thing as 'Sunday best' anymore. So many men and women seem to wear jeans all the while; fewer and fewer people are working yet more and more people are wearing overalls. It doesn't make sense.

A couple of Easters ago, I was in Kialisha, an African township just outside Cape Town. Over a million black South Africans live there in tiny, two-roomed houses, some of which are brick-built but many of which are just sheds with corrugated-iron roofs. Easter Day dawned and from these hovels emerged immaculately dressed adults and children, young girls with bright ribbons in their hair, boys with faces that shone and teeth that gleamed. White shirts and white dresses were the order of the day, white as an archangel's wing. When you consider the poverty, the living conditions and the shortage of water, you just marvel at the determination of these people to look their best for their Lord. Yes, the church was packed, yes, the singing was magnificent. And so was the movement; they can't keep still when they sing. The whole congregation was on the move the moment the music began.

Does God care what we wear in church? Is our being there the most important thing? When we dress up are we doing so for God's benefit, for our own benefit or to impress the rest of the congregation?

'Why do we always dress up, Mom, when
we're only going to pray?'
'Well, it's nice to look your best, love, and
think what the neighbours might say.'
'But does God care what you're wearing? My
friends call me a sissy and laugh.'
'No, I don't think God minds really, as long
as we tread the right path.
But church is a place that's special, it's God's
house and when we are there
Dress is our way of showing respect, love, and
letting Him know that we care.'

3

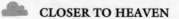

Suffer from Little Children

WHILE DOING PANTO in Southampton, I went to mass at a church I'd never been to before. It was packed and the majority of the congregation were young families. The noise was unbelievable: screaming babies, toddlers using the altar steps as a bouncy castle and five- to eight-year-olds treating the whole place as an adventure playground. I mentioned this on *Good Morning Sunday* the following Sunday and the guest I had on that week, Moira Anderson, stated that children should not even be allowed in church until they were of an age to behave. Letters arrived by the sackful; our postman was issued with a JCB. Many letters agreed with Moira, saying that the church service was a time for communing with God, for meditation and prayer in peaceful surroundings. Others fiercely opposed Moira, saying that if we wished children to become lifelong Christians, the earlier they were taken to church the better.

I'm not usually a neutral but I must confess to

having a bum full of splinters from sitting on the fence in this case until I was swayed by a poem from a regular *GMS* listener, Freda Jones.

*If God could choose a special age at which He'd
      like to be,*
*I think He'd like to be a child, a little child like
      me.*
*He'd understand my feelings when I come into
      His house*
*And not expect me to behave just like a little
      mouse.*
*He knows that I am happiest when I can make a
      noise*
*And share my happy little thoughts with other
      girls and boys.*
*And though we do not know the words to pray or
      even sing*
The patter of my little feet to Him I gladly bring.
*So if sometimes I might offend or, dare I say,
      appal,*
*I know He'd rather have my noise than not have
      me at all.*

Excuses

MY TWO GRANDDAUGHTERS – Gracie who's seven and Francesca who's four – have been taken to church every week since they were born. When they meet someone new, they invariably ask them, 'Which church do you go to?'

Often the answer comes back, 'I don't go to church.'

'Why?' is every child's favourite word, there's no point giving a reason because they'll just say 'why?' again.

Over the years I've heard so many reasons why people don't go to church that I thought I'd give you ten reasons why I never wash …

1 Well, you see I was forced to wash when I was a child, it put me off.
2 I think that people who wash look down on other people, they reckon they're cleaner than the rest of us.
3 There are so many different kinds of soap. I'd

get confused. I could never decide which was
the right one.

4 I used to wash when I was young but it got ever
so boring so I stopped.

5 I still wash on special occasions like Christmas
and Easter, surely that's enough.

6 None of my friends wash.

7 I'm still young. As I get older and I'm a lot
dirtier I'll probably start washing then.

8 I really don't have the time.

9 The bathroom is never warm enough.

10 People who make soap are only after your
money.

Write in the space below your own reason for not
washing and see if it holds water.

God's Painter

TRADESMEN ARE in great demand. If you're a builder, a plumber or an electrician, you'll never starve. A certain tradesman, a painter called Harry, was very keen to make an extra few bob where he could. To this end he'd often thin down paint to make it go a little bit further.

As it happened, he got away with this for some time but eventually a church decided to do a big restoration job on the painting of one of their biggest churches.

Harry put in a bid and, because his price was so low, he got the job.

He set to erecting the trestles, setting up the planks and buying the paint and – I'm sorry to say – thinning it down with the turpentine.

Harry worked hard up on the scaffolding, his little brush was a blur. The job was all but completed when, suddenly, there was a horrendous clap of thunder, the sky opened and rain poured down, washing the thinned paint from all over the church and knocking Harry clear off the scaffold to land on the lawn. Lying there among the gravestones, surrounded by telltale puddles of thinned and useless paint, Harry faced reality. He knew this was a judgment from the Almighty so he got on his knees and cried: 'Oh, God! Forgive me! What should I do?'

And from the thunder spake a mighty voice: 'Repaint! Repaint! And thin no more!'

PRAYER

Go on – Ask

PRAYER IS EVER so important. I've had letters, you know, complaining that I've trivialised prayer; listeners telling me that I should only pray for the important things: world peace, the starving in Africa. OK, they've got a point, but I have to confess that I've been known to pray for a parking space. Are you disgusted by that confession or do you do that too? 'Lay your petitions before me,' He said, and I do.

Can you pray too much and too often? Is God in heaven thinking, 'Oh, no, it's him again'?

I'd hate the Lord to think of me as a pest. If He's all-knowing then surely we need to pray only once

10

for what we want, but we constantly pray the same prayer over and over, especially if it's for someone who's seriously ill. Does God need reminding every day? And what do you say to those people who tell you, 'I don't pray, He never answers anyway'? Try quoting the words of this Garth Brooks song.

Sometimes I thank God for unanswered
*   prayers,*
Remember when you're talking to the man
*   upstairs*
Just because He doesn't answer, doesn't mean
*   He don't care*
Some of God's greatest gifts are unanswered
*   prayers.*

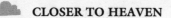

Not Yet

EILEEN McBRIDE, a listener from Glasgow, wrote to me reminding us that although it seems that God leaves prayer unanswered, His answer might be staring us in the face. This is what Eileen had to say:

> *I was always taught that we can ask God for things. He sometimes says 'yes', sometimes says 'no', but sometimes He says 'not yet'. I can live with 'yes' and 'no' but I find the 'not yet' a bit scary sometimes. Imagine waking up one morning, aged forty-five, to find the Shetland pony I prayed for when I was six!*

I suppose it's all down to timing, really. God can see things from a distance and with the benefit of living outside time. He can see the past, the present and the future, whereas I'm stuck with the 'now'. Actually I'm glad I can't see into the future because I've got enough on my hands dealing with today!

So from my heavenly Father's point of view, He's

the best one to change a red light to a green one when the time is right. In fact my earthly father was just the same. When I was about six years old, I remember asking Dad if I could carry his big heavy suitcase out from our car one day.

'Not yet, lad,' was his reply.

'Please, please, please,' I urged, and pushed and entreated as best I knew how.

Dad, never one to give in to my persuasions normally, did on this occasion. 'OK, go ahead then, son,' he smiled.

Thrilled, I bent into the boot of the car, grabbed the handle of the old leather suitcase and went to lift it out. Of course I couldn't. Seeing my dad plucking the suitcase effortlessly in and out of the car time after time, I assumed it was easy but it wasn't. It was simply too heavy and I was too young to carry the weight.

A few years later when I had grown a little and my muscles had taken shape, Dad suddenly turned to me having arrived back from a family holiday and said, 'How about unloading the suitcase for us then, Don?'

I grinned and lifted the case out of the boot and back into our house with ease. The timing was now right as my father knew it would be one day.

Now whenever my heavenly Father says, 'Not yet, Don', I remember why.

Only the Best

I reckon He knows what's best for us. Whenever I ask Him for something, I always add at the end, 'Thy will be done', knowing that God is more likely than anyone to sing back to me ... 'I did it my way.'

> *I asked for Strength ... and God gave me*
>   *Difficulties to make me strong.*
> *I asked for Wisdom ... and God gave me*
>   *Problems to solve.*
> *I asked for Prosperity ... and God gave me*
>   *Brain and Brawn to work.*
> *I asked for Courage ... and God gave me*
>   *Danger to overcome.*
> *I asked for Love ... and God gave me*
>   *Troubled People to help.*
> *I asked for Favours ... and God gave me*
>   *Opportunities.*
> *I got nothing I wanted ... and yet I received*
>   *everything I needed!*

Help Me Pray, Lord

We thank you, Father, for the gift of prayer
Thank you that we are able to communicate
*   directly with you,*
The Lord of all creation.
Help all those of us who find prayer difficult.
Give us the ability to concentrate.
Remove all distraction from our minds and,
When we plead for Your intervention, Lord,
Remind us to always include the words …
'Thy Will Be Done.'
Amen.

Prayer for Our World

Thank you, Lord, for all the diverse wonders
  of the world.
We know that everything, even the air that
  we breathe, comes from you.
Guide us in our efforts to be good custodians
  of the planet that you have entrusted to
  our care.
Help us to realise that the resources of the
  planet
  are for the benefit of all people,
  not just of the few.
Amen.

Out of My Control

JOHN DENVER longed to travel in space, he told me. He was always eager to talk about flying,

'So, you've got a Tomahawk,' he said. 'Great plane.'

'What have you got?' I asked.

'A Pitts Special [fully aerobatic biplane] and a Lear Jet,' he replied.

That meant that he was in the Premiership while I was in the Conference League but he didn't see it like that. To him I was a fellow pilot and he treated me as such. Sadly he died at the controls of an experimental light aircraft but somehow I think that's the way he would have wanted to go.

On a trip to Northern France, I stopped at Wavans Commonwealth War Grave Commission cemetery. I wanted to visit the grave of James McCudden, VC, one of the great flying heroes of the First World War. There was an inscription on the gravestone, put there by his parents who had lost both their other sons flying with the RFC in the conflict. I think it would look good at John Denver's resting place.

> *Fly on dear boy*
> *from this dark world of strife*
> *on to the promised land*
> *to eternal life.*

Eugene

MUCH TO THE distress of my mother, I attended a non-Catholic primary school. Places in Roman Catholic schools were at a premium when I was five and I couldn't get one. From the age of seven, however, I attended religious instruction classes every Saturday morning at St John's Convent where I was taught my faith by a lovely nun called Sister Annuncia.

Once there I fell under the influence of Eugene who was a year older than me. He was a big lad with ginger hair and lots of freckles and while I was a bit of a goody-goody, Eugene was always up to mischief. One Monday he stole a bit of 'blue bag' from his mother's washing. He stored it carefully. Then, on Sunday morning, he made sure he was late for nine o'clock mass. Everyone was already inside so they didn't see him drop the blue bag into the holy water font. Eugene was first out of mass at the end. He wanted to witness all the grown-ups as they left church, each with a big blue spot on forehead and chest.

Eugene had another little wheeze. He'd put an Elastoplast, sticky-side out, on his middle finger. Then, when the plate came round, he'd flick his finger into it and, instead of depositing a coin, he'd come out with a sixpence.

Inventive as he was when it came to being naughty, he had a great interest in prayer, though he had his own version of most things: 'Our Father who art in heaven, Harold be thy name.'

'It's not "Harold", it's "hallowed",' I explained.

'No such word,' replied Eugene. 'God's Christian name is "Harold".'

'God doesn't have a Christian name.'

'He does then, see. Jesus is His son and Jesus is a Christian so it stands to reason, His Dad must be a Christian too and if He's a Christian he's gorra have a Christian name and He has. His name's Harold.'

He then progressed to the 'Hail Mary', which he loved. Eugene spent most Saturday afternoons at Moseley Road Baths. He wasn't well off like me. He didn't have a woolly cossie that had been lovingly knitted by his mom. He had to hire 'slips' – so-called because, as you walked, certain bits of you

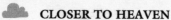

'slipped' out – but he loved the baths. He'd emerge after several hours smelling of chlorine and looking like a bloodshot-eyed prune. He developed a particular devotion for the Blessed Virgin Mary because of the words of her prayer: 'Hail Mary, full of grace, the Lord is with thee, blessed art thou a monk swimming.'

We tried to correct him but he wouldn't have it. As far as he was concerned it was 'Harold be Thy name', 'Blessed art thou a monk swimming' and 'Glory be to the Father and to the Son and to the Only Goat'.

Growin' Old

I'VE NOW REACHED the age when everything I've got aches and if it don't ache, it don't work. I mentioned this to someone of a similar age the other day. She said, 'I know exactly what you mean. I woke up the other morning and nothing was aching. For a moment I thought I must have died during the night.'

Sheila Birkett from Shipley in West Yorkshire sent me this lovely prayer:

> *Lord, look kindly down on me*
> *Now I am past my best,*
> *Remember please my gammy knee*
> *And my worn and wheezy chest.*
> *Remember too my failing sight,*
> *My bones and joints that creak,*
> *The hours of sleep I miss at night*
> *That make me feel antique.*
> *And not forgetting other parts*
> *That now are going too,*

CLOSER TO HEAVEN

Please make sure the door's unlocked
When I need to use the loo.
Please let me still appreciate
All the joys of life
Books and music, theatre, art
Oh and don't forget the wife.
Keep my old heart ticking
At a nice and steady pace
But when it's time to stop dear Lord
Grant that I may see Your face.

Resignation

I HAVE DECIDED that I'd quite like to be a child again. It has its problems but it's a lot better than being a grown-up so I now offer this resignation:

Dear God,
I am hereby officially tendering my resigna-
tion as an adult. I have decided I would like
to accept the responsibilities of a six-year-old
again. I want to go to McDonald's and think
that it's a four-star restaurant. I want to sail
sticks across a fresh mud puddle and make
ripples with rocks. I want to think chocolate
buttons are better than money because you
can eat them.

I want to lie under a big oak tree and
drink lemonade with my friends on a hot
summer's day. I want to return to a time
when life was simple – a time when all you
knew were colours, multiplication tables and
nursery rhymes but that didn't bother you

*because you didn't know what you didn't
know and you didn't care that you didn't
know things. All you cared about was being
happy because you were blissfully unaware of
all the things that should make you worried
or upset.*

*I want to believe that the world is fair,
that everyone is honest and good. I want to
believe that anything is possible. I want to be
oblivious to the complexities of life and be
overly excited by the little things again. I
want things to be simple. I don't want my
day to consist of computer crashes, mountains
of paperwork, depressing news, worrying
about how to survive more days in the month
than there is money in the bank, bills, gossip,
illness and loss of loved ones.*

*I want to believe in the power of smiles,
hugs, a kind word, truth, justice, peace,
dreams, the imagination, mankind and
making angels in the snow. So here's my
chequebook and my car keys, my credit card
and my bank statements. I am officially*

resigning from adulthood. And if you want to discuss this further, God, you'll have to catch me first, 'cos, 'Tag! You're it!'

I tell you the truth, anyone who will not receive the kingdom of God like a little child will never enter it.

MARK 10:15

God on the Line

IN THE OLD TESTAMENT, God was always turning up. All the prophets either saw Him or heard from Him. He parted seas, dropped manna from heaven, showered Egypt with frogs and made sure everyone had a boil for good measure but He's been a bit quiet lately, hasn't He?

I know a few people who say they've heard from God. I know a bloke named Mike who actually saw God – mind, he had died for a few moments before paramedics dragged him back to this life.

I'm jealous of such people. They've heard from God. Why haven't I? Why doesn't God want to talk to me? Are we all too sophisticated and cynical nowadays, would we know if God was trying to contact us? I doubt it, we'd dismiss it as imagination or static electricity. I was fascinated therefore to read the following. It's from the United States and it's entitled simply 'Does God Still Speak to Us?'

A young man had been to Wednesday night

Bible study. The pastor had spoken about listening to God and obeying the Lord's voice. The young man couldn't help but wonder, 'Does God still speak to people?' After service he went out with some friends for coffee and pie and they discussed the message. Several different ones talked about how God had led them in different ways. It was about ten o'clock when the young man started driving home. Sitting in his car, he just began to pray, 'God, if you still speak to people, speak to me. I will listen. I will do my best to obey.'

As he drove down the main street of his town, he had the strangest thought, to stop and buy a gallon of milk. He shook his head and said out loud, 'God, is that you?' He didn't get a reply and started on toward home. But again, the thought, buy a gallon of milk. The young man thought about Samuel and how he didn't recognise the voice of God, and how little Samuel ran to Eli. 'OK, God, in case that is you, I will buy the milk.'

It didn't seem like too hard a test of

obedience. He could always use the milk. He stopped and purchased the gallon of milk and started off toward home. As he passed Seventh Street, he again felt the urge, 'Turn down that street.'

'This is crazy,' he thought and drove on past the intersection. Again, he felt that he should turn down Seventh Street. At the next intersection, he turned back and headed down Seventh. Half jokingly, he said out loud, 'OK, God, I will.' He drove several blocks, when suddenly he felt like he should stop. He pulled over to the kerb and looked around. He was in a semicommercial area of town. It wasn't the best, but it wasn't the worst of neighbourhoods either.

The businesses were closed and most of the houses looked dark, as though the people were already in bed. Again, he sensed something, 'Go and give the milk to the people in the house across the street.'

The young man looked at the house. It was dark and it looked as if the people were either away or they were already asleep. He started to open the door and then sat back in the car seat. 'Lord, this is insane. Those people are asleep and if I wake them up, they are going to be mad and I will look stupid.'

Again, he felt he should go and give the milk. Finally, he opened the door, 'OK, God, if this is you, I will go to the door and I will give them the milk. If you want me to look like a crazy person, OK. I want to be obedient. I guess that will count for something but if they don't answer right away, I'm out of here.'

He walked across the street and rang the bell. He could hear some noise inside. A man's voice yelled out, 'Who is it? What do you want?' Then the door opened before the young man could get away. A man was standing there in his jeans and T-shirt. He looked like he just got out of bed. He had a strange look on his face and he didn't seem too happy to have some stranger standing on his doorstep. 'What is it?'

The young man thrust out the gallon of milk, 'Here, I brought this to you.'

31

The man took the milk and rushed down a hallway speaking loudly in Spanish. Then from down the hall came a woman carrying the milk toward the kitchen. The man was following her, holding a baby. The baby was crying. The man had tears streaming down his face. The man began speaking and half crying, 'We were just praying. We had some big bills this month and we ran out of money. We didn't have any milk for our baby. I was just praying and asking God to show me how to get some milk.'

His wife in the kitchen yelled out, 'I ask him to send an angel with some. Are you an angel?'

The young man reached into his wallet and pulled out all the money he had on him and put it in the man's hand. He turned and walked back toward his car and the tears were streaming down his face. He knew that God still answers prayers.

'God, if you still speak to people, speak to me, I will listen and obey.'

PRAYER

ASAP

ASAP OFTEN says 'as soon as possible' but it doesn't have to mean that as Etty Messam told me:

> *There's work to do, deadlines to meet,*
> *You've got no time to spare*
> *But as you hurry and scurry*
> *ASAP – Always say a prayer.*
> *In the midst of family chaos*
> *Quality time is rare,*
> *Do your best, God'll do the rest*
> *If you ASAP – Always say a prayer.*
> *It may seem that your worries*
> *Are more than you can bear*
> *Slow down, take a breather,*
> *ASAP – Always say a prayer.*
> *God knows how stressful life is,*
> *He wants to ease our cares,*
> *He'll respond to all your needs*
> *ASAP – Always say a prayer.*

PEOPLE

Heroes

I WENT TO BERLIN last September, on one of those cheapie flights from Stanstead. There was much I wanted to see in this city, which had been flattened by Bomber Command, rebuilt, then divided by an abomination of a wall. The Berlin Wall came down in 1989 and only small bits of it remain as a reminder. I was on a pilgrimage of sorts. Claus von Stauffenberg is a great hero of mine, in fact I consider him to be the greatest hero of the Second World War. If you're struggling to remember exactly who he was, let me remind you. He was the officer who planted the bomb intended to kill Hitler on 20 July 1944. That same night, he was arrested and, with three others, was shot in the courtyard of the Bendler Block.

I set off on foot to see the place where my hero had met his end. The road leading to it has now been renamed Stauffenbergstrasse and the Bendler Block now houses the Museum of Resistance to National Socialism, proof that the Germans too acknowledge the greatness of the man. Not so the British press. On the fiftieth anniversary of the July '44 Plot, which was 1994 [you could have worked that out for yourself, couldn't you?], several newspapers described Stauffenberg as 'a disaffected Nazi'. Nothing could be further from the truth. I wrote letters to all the editors informing them that the conspirators did as they did because of their religious beliefs.

One of his fellow conspirators, Major General Henning von Tresckow said,

God once promised Abraham not to destroy Sodom if only ten righteous people could be found. I hope that, because of us, God will not destroy Germany. The moral value of a

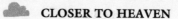

*human being begins only at the point at
which he is willing to give his life for his con-
viction.*

I was determined to visit the Roman Catholic cathedral, St Hedwig's, in Berlin. To do so I had to walk
through the square where thousands of books were
burned by Nazis in a frenzy of hate merely because
their authors were Jewish. Throughout the war,
Konrad von Preysing was the Bishop of Berlin.
Apparently Stauffenberg went to see him at St
Hedwig's Cathedral before the assassination
attempt; he wanted to know that killing the tyrant
would not deny him entry into paradise when his
time came. Stauffenberg was seeking absolution
before the event. Obviously this couldn't be given.
However, the bishop told him that he honoured his
motives and did not regard himself as justified in
attempting to restrain him on theological grounds.

Stauffenberg paid with his life. There is a plaque
on the wall in the courtyard where he and three
others faced a firing squad on 20 July 1944. I
prayed there for the repose of his soul.

PEOPLE

Out of the depths I have cried to Thee, O Lord. Lord, hear my voice. If Thine ears be attentive to the voice of my supplication, Lord, I shall endure it. For with the Lord there is mercy and with Him plentiful redemption, and He shall redeem Israel for all its iniquities. Eternal rest grant unto him, O Lord, and let perpetual light shine upon him. May he rest in peace.

Was Claus von Stauffenberg a martyr? I think he was but you'll have to make up your own mind.

Jozy Pollock

I RECENTLY interviewed Jozy Pollock, a fascinating woman. Born in England, she'd met and married Channing Pollock who was the greatest stage magician of his generation. She'd gone back to the States with him and worked as his assistant, appearing on stage in Las Vegas and regularly on coast-to-coast television. She was glamorous in the extreme, she partied with the rich and the famous, her friends were film stars and politicians but she was unfulfilled. She sold her jewellery piece by piece and gave the money to the poor. In 1984, inspired by Isaiah 42:7 – 'to open eyes that are blind, to free captives from prison and to release from the dungeon those who sit in darkness' – she was accepted to serve as a prison chaplain, finally becoming ordained in 1990.

'Never doubt that God has a sense of humour,' Jozy said to me.

I've seen demons manifest in men's bodies.
Men growling and cursing, trying to urinate

on me so when, one day, I came to a cell and the man inside said, 'Hello my sweet angel, how are you?' it was a pleasant surprise.

'I'm fine,' I replied. 'Do you know Jesus?'

The man smiled, 'I am Jesus.'

When I doubted him, he ordered me out of 'his' jail. I continued talking to him though, he rather amused me. He reminded me of a leprechaun: rosy cheeks, blue eyes, grey hair standing up on end and a thick Irish brogue. I'd known a few drunken, Irish actors in my time, many of them could have ended up like this. I continued my walk along the row but, on the way back, I decided to ask him one last question: 'If you're who you say you are, why don't you escape?'

'Do you mind! I've come in here for a rest. It's chaos out there, I need to regroup.' I guess he wasn't crazy after all.

Sex Symbol

IT'S OFTEN been said that I'm a sex symbol for women of a certain age. I take that as a compliment. I don't suppose it's possible to be a sex symbol for nuns, that would be a contradiction in terms, but there are a lot of reverend ladies in convents around the country who listen to my dulcet tones on a Sunday. I'm always pleased to receive communications from them. Sister Pauline who's now at St Joseph's Convent in Wolverhampton sent me this a few weeks ago:

> *Let me introduce you to some of the members of our community, all of them have the same surname 'Tate'. First there's Sister Dic Tate who wants to run everything, then there's Sister Ro Tate who wants to change everything.*
>
> *Sister Agi Tate constantly stirs up trouble with the help of Sister Irri Tate. Whenever there are new projects suggested Sister Hesi Tate wants to wait until next year and Sister*

Vege Tate wants to leave things as they are.

Then there's Sister Imi Tate who wants our community to be like the motherhouse. Sister Devas Tate provides the voice of doom while Sister Poten Tate just wants to be a big shot.

But there's also Sister Facili Tate who's always about when there's work to be done and Sister Cogi Tate and Sister Medi Tate who always think things over and are positive in their ideas, unlike Sister Decapi Tate who keeps losing her head and Sister Levi Tate who's always up in the air.

Our hypochondriac, Sister Premedi Tate, takes medicine before there's anything wrong with her but Sister Regurgi Tate keeps bringing it back. All this is most confusing for Sister Orien Tate who's on loan to us from China but happily, Sister Gravi Tate draws everyone to her and Sister Reins Tate puts everyone back in their place.

All in all we're a happy bunch except for Sister Ampu Tate who's sadly cut herself off completely from the rest of the community.

Heart of the Matter

INEVITABLY I'M often asked, 'Who is the most interesting person you've ever interviewed?' Difficult one to answer, that. I did, though, on three occasions interview Professor Christiaan Barnard. During my interview with the doctor I could have been overawed to be in the presence of one of only two men from my lifespan whom I can guarantee will still be an encyclopaedia entry one thousand years from now, the other one being Neil Armstrong of course. Professor Barnard was a great interviewee, full of fun and seemingly fit as a flea when I last interviewed him in May 2001. Sadly it was the last interview he gave to anyone – he died a few days later.

He was a man of great faith, you know. His father was a minister of the Dutch Reformed Church and his mother played the organ at the services. She was a bit deaf and, as a young boy, Christiaan stood at her side and nudged her to tell her when to start the hymn. He was also responsible for pumping the bellows. He prayed before every operation. He told me the prayer he said before he removed the heart from the car-crash victim Denise Duvall and transplanted it into the chest cavity of Louis Washkansky:

> *Lord, guide my hands tonight. Keep them*
> *free from error as You have freed me from*
> *doubt and shown me the way to do this as well*
> *as I can for this brave man who has placed his*
> *life in my hands.*

'Were you playing God at that moment?' I asked him.

'No, but I was doing God's work,' he replied. 'Any advance, scientific or medical, is a revelation from God. If He didn't want us to use it, it wouldn't be revealed to us.'

I imagine many people would struggle with that statement but Christiaan Barnard firmly believed it.

Whenever I think of him, I remember how he described replacing one person's failing heart with another that would bring new life. While I'm astounded at how much of a miracle this was, it seemed to be so matter-of-fact for him.

So it is for God who, when we come to him, replaces our old nature with one filled with his spirit. However, just like being a patient of Dr Christiaan Barnard, we need to trust the heavenly surgeon's knife.

> *The longest distance in the world is the length between a person's head and their heart.*
>
> AUTHOR UNKNOWN

Thousands of transplants have now been performed. At Southwark Cathedral each year, there's a special service in memory of all those who donate their body parts to medical science. I was most alarmed when I attended one of these services and, according to the service sheet, was invited to stay behind at the end for a finger buffet!

Biodots

WHILE ENTERTAINING on a P&O cruise, I attended several lectures given by a fascinating and very humorous woman, Diane Simpson. In one of the lectures she gave each of us a biodot, which we were to stick onto our hand. These biodots monitor skin temperature fluctuations, which are due to changes in the amount of blood flowing through the skin. If you're tense, skin bloodflow is reduced and the biodot will turn yellow, amber or black but when you're calm, the biodot will be turquoise, blue or violet. So black = very tense, while violet = very relaxed. Mine never went below green which is defined as 'involved and alert'. I don't think I'm stressed but I certainly don't relax, I want to be doing something. If I'm watching TV, I'm doing something else at the same time; writing, reading, crossword-solving.

The French philosopher Blaise Pascal said that all our worries would be over if we spent a small time each day alone with our thoughts.

So how do I relax? Easy, I fly aeroplanes. The concentration needed in the cockpit of a light aircraft, especially in marginal weather, is so great that you are unable to think of anything else and that's relaxing.

When you first sit in a cockpit confronted by eight clocks, none of which are telling the same time, half a steering wheel and no clutch, you think: 'I'll never get the hang of this' but, after a short time, you find that with one glance, your brain can take in the information from all eight dials that confront you. You also get to understand what the controller is saying to you on the radio once you realise that he always says things in exactly the same order.

So what's so wonderful about flying? I could never hope to put that into words, but someone did. His name was Pilot Officer Gillespie Magee of 412 Squadron RCAF. He was killed in action on 11 December 1941 but he left this poem – *High Flight* – so that those who have never flown solo can know just how it feels.

PEOPLE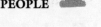

Oh I have slipped the surly bonds of Earth
And danced the skies on laughter-silvered
    wings.
Sunward I've climbed and joined the
    tumbling mirth
Of sun-split clouds and done a hundred
    things
You have not dreamed of – wheeled and
    soared and swung
High in the sunlit silence.
Hovering there, I've chased the shouting
    wind along and flung
My eager craft through footless halls of air
Up, up the long delirious burning blue.
I've topped the windswept heights with easy
    grace
Where never lark nor even eagle flew
And while with silent lifting mind I've trod
The high untrespassed sanctity of space,
Put out my hand and touched the face of
    God.

Mind the Trap

TRAPDOORS ARE a nightmare. Last Christmas I played Widow Twanky in *Aladdin* at the Birmingham Hippodrome. We had a genie of the ring, the delightful Amanda Barrie who was recently deceased from *Coronation Street*. The times Abanazar stood on stage in a cloud of smoke, rubbing his ring and waiting for Amanda to shoot up from the bowels of this trap!

One evening, Bobby Davro [my boy Aladdin] and I were on stage. He rubbed the ring, there was a huge flash and Amanda started her upward journey by trap. Suddenly there was a clunk, the trap lift stopped and all we could see of our genie was her head and shoulders, enshrouded in smoke, protruding from the stage.

'I can't for the life of me remember leaving that in the oven,' I ad-libbed and Bobby and I set about lifting the genie onto the stage. A little while later someone told me this true story which makes my ad-lib pale into insignificance by comparison.

PEOPLE

A church drama group presented a play in which, during the first act, one character would stand on a trapdoor and announce, 'I descend into hell!' A stagehand below would then pull a rope, the trapdoor would open and the character would plunge through. The play was to run for a week but, on the second night, the actor playing the part was taken ill. Bill, one of the stage crew, agreed to do the part but, as the performance was already underway, there was no time to rehearse. What I've not mentioned is that Bill was a big lad, he'd obviously been made when meat was cheap.

At the appointed time, he stood on the trapdoor and announced: 'I descend into hell!' The stagehand pulled the rope and Bill began his plunge but they'd reckoned without Bill's girth. He became hopelessly stuck. The stagehand grabbed his legs from below but that only made things worse. No amount of tugging would pull him through. When all seemed lost, Bill came up with his inspired ad-lib: Hallelujah!' he cried. 'Hell is full!'

MONEY

Filthy Lucre

AH, MONEY, the root of all evil. A fool and his money are soon parted but, hang on, how did a fool and his money get together in the first place?

Money is not the key to happiness. No, but if you've got enough of it, you can get a key cut. I grew up in the 1950s when a lad was judged by how he treated people younger than himself and also those older. Good works and good manners afforded him kudos. Now a lad is judged by the size of his car and his bank balance and the make of trainers he wears. So is money really that important?

An old boy of a good Catholic school who had

done rather well for himself in the City met another old boy who happened to be training for the priesthood.

'How much money do you have in the bank?' he asked.

'I don't know. I've not shaken it lately,' came the reply.

Perhaps we put too much emphasis on money and lose focus on the things that pounds cannot buy, like friendship, family and faith.

Money Isn't Everything

HERE'S A Cree Indian prophecy for you:

> *Only after the last tree has been cut down,*
> *Only after the last river has been poisoned,*
> *Only after the last fish has been caught,*
> *Only then will you find that money cannot*
> *be eaten.*

Let's Play

EVERY KID I know has got a computer and a mountain bike but what do they say all day long? 'I'm bored, I'm ever so bored, never bin so bored, I'm really bored I am!'

We weren't bored and we played with things that cost nothing. I used to put my hand inside my shirt, trap air under my arm and, by moving my elbow up and down, play a tune – who needs a Nintendo when you've got an armpit? I even had a flea circus till my mom stopped me playing with the boy next door – it cost nothing.

Toys were hard to come by just after the Second World War. My dad made me a fort for Christmas. He made it out of firewood and he painted it red and green which was the only paint he could get. I had so much enjoyment out of that fort despite the fact that I got splinters in my hands every time I played with it. See, it wasn't that my parents couldn't afford toys, there were just none about. Now I walk into Toys R Us and marvel at the wonders filling every shelf, but are they any more appreciated than my fort, my armpit or the old tin bath which me and my mates turned into an armoured car, a covered wagon and a submarine?

A word of wisdom for all toy buyers: 'The best toys are powered by imagination, not by batteries.'

All the Rage

MY WIFE TONI and I went into Curry's to look at televisions the other day. They're all silver! I called over the assistant, an Asian lad with one lowered eyebrow which marked him out as a member of the computer generation, skilled in the command functions of every piece of electrical equipment in this warehouse and beyond.

'They're all silver,' I began.

'Yes,' he confirmed. He couldn't very well deny it. They were shining like a row of aluminium dustbins.

'We were looking for a dark one. You know, black or brown.'

'You won't find a black television these days. You see, silver is the new black.'

'Eh!' We didn't see so we left. We popped next door to B&Q. In the bathroom department I remarked, 'All the toilets, baths, sinks are white. What happened to coloured bathroom suites?'

A passing assistant, overhearing my remark,

handed me an opened catalogue. 'White is the new avocado,' she said by way of explanation.

By now we were both well confused. We returned to the car park. It was easy to find our car, it was the only red one there.

'I remember when nearly all cars were red,' said Toni. 'Now most cars are silver.'

'It's to match the TV sets,' I said.

'Either that or silver is the new red,' she said. We both fell about laughing, it was getting ridiculous now.

I've always had red cars, I just like red. For most people red means stop but not for me. In my case it's hot, it's fast, it's encouraging me to go – yes, you've guessed it, for me red is the new green.

Once in the car I switched on Radio 2, as you do. They were discussing age and we heard the presenter say, 'Sixty is the new forty'. Now I understood that. We used to say, 'Life begins at forty' but because of better food, better healthcare and more exercise, life now begins at sixty.

Thank goodness that God is the same yesterday, today and forever!

Putting Problems into Perspective

IF YOU HAVE never experienced the danger of battle, the loneliness of imprisonment, the agony of torture or the pangs of starvation, you are ahead of 500 hundred million people in the world.

If you can attend a church without fear of harassment, arrest, torture or death, you are more blessed than 3 billion people in the world.

If you have food to eat, clothes on your back, a roof over your head and some money in the bank, you are among the top 8 per cent of the world's wealthiest people.

And if you're reading this, you are more blessed than 2 billion people in the world who cannot read at all.

LIFE AND DEATH

It's a Gift

Each life is indeed a gift
No matter how short
No matter how fragile.
Each life is indeed a gift
To be held in our hearts forever.

Grandma's Stocking

THIS LOVELY POEM that was sent to me reminds us that it's best that we don't know the future, but just trust God for today.

'Gran'ma look into the future
Tell me what will happen in my life.
Will I be rich, will I be happy,
Will I become somebody's wife?'
Gran'ma put down her knitting
And lifted me onto her knee.
I rested my head on her bosom
And these are the words she said to me.
'My child, life is a stocking
In your case, it has just begun
But I am now knitting the toe of mine
'Cos my work on Earth's almost done.
The stocking will change as you grow, dear,
Living your life day to day.
Some parts will be bright, bright colours
Others will be deathly grey.

Most parts will be smooth and even
But sometimes a stitch you will drop.
You'll pick up and carry on knitting
'Cos this stocking you just cannot stop.
There'll be long, plain dull stretches
There'll be others exciting and dear
I can see a few bumpy patches
Some of them stained with a tear.
When you've finished the heel, my darling,
There'll be just the foot left to do
You'll look back over your knitting
I hope what you see pleases you.
Just the toe left to knit and you're finished
Your stocking is almost spun,
Your heavenly Father can now break the
        thread
And say, "Come home, your work here is
        done."

Whatever Life Throws at Me

It cannot shatter my love.
It cannot eradicate my hope.
It cannot corrode my faith.
It cannot eat away my peace.
It cannot destroy my confidence.
It cannot invade my soul.
It cannot quench my spirit.
It cannot lessen the power of the
    resurrection.
It cannot reduce my hope of eternal life.

Life Explained

CAN YOU IMAGINE the scene if creation had negotiated its own existence? God still has the last laugh though!

On the first day God created the cow. God said to the cow, 'You must spend all day under the sun in the field where you will eat grass, chew the cud, have calves and give milk to feed the calves and to support the farmer. For this I shall give you a life span of sixty years.'

'That's a long time to endure such a hard life, Lord,' said the cow. 'Let me have just twenty years, I'll give back the other forty.' And God agreed.

On the second day, God created the dog. God said to the dog, 'Sit all day by the door of your house and bark at anyone who comes in or walks past. For this I shall give you a life span of twenty years.'

'That's a long time to be barking,' said the dog. 'Let me have just ten years, I'll give back the other ten.' And God agreed.

On the third day, God created the monkey. God said to the monkey, 'Entertain people, do monkey tricks, make everybody laugh. For this I shall give you a twenty-year life span.'

'Monkey tricks for twenty years?' said the monkey. 'Make people laugh for twenty years? No chance. The dog gave you back ten years so I'll do the same. I'll be quite happy with just ten years.' And God agreed.

On the fourth day God created man. God said to man, 'Eat and drink, sleep, play, enjoy yourself. Do nothing, just enjoy life. For this I shall give you a twenty-year life span.'

Man said, 'What! Only twenty years? That's not enough. Tell you what, I'll take my twenty plus the forty the cow gave back plus the ten the monkey gave back plus the ten the dog gave back. That makes eighty – OK?'

'OK by me,' said God, 'I agree.'

And that's why for the first twenty years of our lives we eat, sleep, play and enjoy ourselves, do nothing, just enjoy life; for the next forty years we slave in the sun to support our family; for the next ten years we do monkey tricks to entertain the grandchildren and for the last ten years we sit in front of the house and bark at everyone. Life has now been explained.

Bow and Exit Left

I SOMETIMES WONDER how I'll take my final bow here on Earth. I think I'd rather die suddenly and without any pain but at least I know that however I leave this world, I shall arrive at the next one with a shout of joy. It's this thought that takes away the sting of death for those who believe.

The 'how' and 'where' is out of my control but it's in the hands of someone I trust, Who not only walks with me in the light of life but in the shadow of death as well.

Whenever I get a bit concerned about my earthly departure, I pray this comforting prayer:

> *Dear God,*
> *help me not to be so concerned*
> *with the passing of this world,*
> *as to looking forward*
> *to arriving at the new.*
> *Amen.*

What Fore?

GOLF HAS ALWAYS been a puzzle to me. I have absolutely no interest in it whatsoever. It has a language all of its own. 'It's a par bird, birdy par, albatross, eagle, bird bogie par.' What does all that mean?

My son-in-law was watching the Ryder Cup on television. As I walked into the room, I heard the commentator say, 'The last four holes were all square.' Square holes! Are they playing with sugar cubes instead of balls? And what's a triple bogie? It doesn't bear thinking about. Having said all of this, I do realise that very many people get great pleasure from the game, it becomes a passion, it takes over their lives.

I've heard chaps say that, if they died on the golf course, they'd die happy. Bing Crosby did just that, dropped down dead while playing golf. His death was the lead item on the news on Radio 2. Hearing it, the producer of the show that was going out at the time grabbed a Bing Crosby CD from the shelf and thrust it at his presenter.

'Play a track from that when the news finishes,' he instructed.

'What track?' asked the presenter.

'Any one'll do as long as it's Bing.'

'"Cheek to cheek"?'

'That'll be fine.' The news finished, the green light flashed.

'Sad to hear of the death of Bing Crosby but he lives on through his music. Here's the Old Groaner with a word for us all.' The presenter pressed the button and on went 'Cheek to cheek', which begins with the words, 'Heaven, I'm in heaven.'

When Bing died, I remember so many people saying, 'What a wonderful way to go', but is it? I recently read a heart-rending book written by an extremely religious young man, Andrew Robinson, who was diagnosed with terminal cancer while studying for the priesthood. He documented the last four months of his life, which he used to make his peace with God. He even managed a pilgrimage to San Giovanni, the shrine to Padre Pio. At his funeral, his father had these words to say:

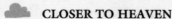

Our precious son has been on loan to us for thirty-one years and it has been a great privilege and joy to be his parents. I think I now have a little understanding of the Jewish custom of offering their first-born to the Lord.

So you have to ask yourself, would you prefer a swift, painless exit from this life or one during which you have time to say goodbye to those you love and to prepare yourself to meet your Maker?

Journey's End

EVERYBODY WANTS TO go to heaven but nobody wants to die.

Tony Blackburn recently decided that he believes in reincarnation so he's made a new will, leaving everything to himself.

A chap having fully embraced the concept of reincarnation decided to join a reincarnation society. Having turned up for the meeting he was informed that the joining fee and yearly membership would be £150.

'A hundred and fifty quid! That's a bit steep,' he complained.

'Oh, come on,' said the society's treasurer, 'you only live once.'

Why are jokes about death so funny? Because we need to laugh at things that scare us and when we do that fear is released.

'How did the funeral go?'

'Oh, it was luverly. The hearse stopped outside and we brought him into the house.'

'You never got a coffin into that little house of yours.'

'Well, not all the way in, we stood it up in the hallway then we took the lid orf so's he could have one larst look round.'

'Oh, that's luverly.'

'Then we toasted his life in Scotch whisky.'

'You didn't.'

'We did – then after six bottles of Scotch whisky, we all went down the cemetery and buried the grandfather clock.'

Victorians never talked about sex but were totally obsessed with death. Now we're obsessed with sex but ncvcr talk about death.

> *May you be in heaven a fortnight before the devil knows you're dead.*
>
> IRISH BLESSING OF SORTS

Struggles

A MAN FOUND A cocoon of a butterfly. One day, a small opening appeared.

The man sat and watched the butterfly for several hours as it struggled to force its body through that little hole.

After a while, the butterfly seemed to stop making any progress. It appeared to have gone as far as it could and could go no further. So, the man decided to help the butterfly; he took a pair of scissors and snipped off the remaining bit of the cocoon.

The butterfly then emerged easily. However, it had a swollen body and small, shrivelled wings. The man continued to watch the butterfly. He expected that, at any moment, the wings would enlarge and expand to be able to support the body which would contract in time. Neither happened! In fact the butterfly spent the rest of its life crawling around with swollen body and shrivelled wings. The butterfly was never able to fly. What the man, in his kindness

71

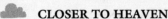

and haste, did not understand was that the restricting cocoon and the struggle required for the butterfly to get through the tiny opening were God's way of forcing fluid from the body of the butterfly into its wings so that it would be ready for flight once it achieved its freedom from the cocoon.

Sometimes struggles are exactly what we need in our lives. If God allowed us to go through our lives without any obstacles, it would cripple us. We would not be as strong as what we could have been. We could never fly!

Numbers Up

Everybody has a favourite number, they say. It's the one you look for when you're buying a raffle ticket. Mine was always eleven. Why's that?

Well, I was born on 11 March, I received the letter telling me I'd passed my eleven-plus on 11 May, I got married on 11 February, I made my first ever television appearance on 11 May. Added to that, I played on the left wing at both soccer and rugby so I had number eleven on my back and my dad always told me that there were eleven commandments. What's the eleventh? 'Thou shalt not be found out', of course.

The number eleven took on great significance at the end of the First World War. All firing ceased at the eleventh hour of the eleventh day of the eleventh month.

The only eleven that ever bothered me was the eleventh station of the cross. It's the one that, even now, I'm drawn to. The Eleventh Station: 'Jesus is nailed to the cross'. It's so barbaric. When I concentrate I can almost hear it. Did He cry out when the nails pierced His hands and His feet? Did He realise then that there was still a further three hours of extreme agony to be endured? He must have done.

Despite that, eleven remained my favourite number. Then came 11 September 2001.

11 September 2001 was a day that none of us living today will ever forget. The following Sunday, letters and e-mails flooded in to the programme.

'Where was God on 11 September?' went up the cry from nearly all our correspondents. Poet and listener Andy George had the answer:

> *Where were you when the planes struck?*
> *Where were you when the buildings shook?*
> *Where were you when the fireball burst?*
> *Where were you when the pain was worst?*
> *Where were you?*
> *I was there on every floor,*
> *I was there when they cried no more,*
> *I was there to love and embrace,*
> *I was there on each tear-stained face,*

I was there.
Where were you when the buildings fell?
Where were you when we knew this hell?
Where were you when the victims cried?
Where were you when the children died?
Where were you?
I was there in the horror and pain,
I was there in both those planes,
I was there in the scorching flame,
I was there to take the blame,
I was there.

ANDY GEORGE

Now the number eleven has more significance for me than ever before.

CLOSER TO HEAVEN

9/11

SHORTLY AFTER 11 September 2001, as a guest on GMS, I had Tom Paxton, the man who was really responsible for getting an entire generation interested in folk music. He'd just written a song about the tragedy which had befallen his beloved New York. There and then he took out his guitar and 'The Bravest' enjoyed its first public performance:

> *I grabbed the pictures from my desk and joined the flight for life*
> *With every step I called the names of my children and my wife*
> *And then we heard them coming up from several floors below*
> *A crowd of fire-fighters with their heavy gear in tow*
> *And now I go to funerals for men I never knew.*
> *The pipers play 'Amazing Grace' as the coffins come in view*

*They must have seen it coming as they turned
to face the fire
They sent us down to safety then they kept on
climbing higher
Now every time I try to sleep, I'm haunted by
the sound
Of firemen climbing up the stairs while we
were running down.*

The bravery of the New York fire-fighters will
ensure that they take their place alongside all the
great heroes of history. They are truly entitled to be
numbered among 'The Bravest'.

*Greater love has no-one than this, that he lay
down his life for his friends.*

JOHN 15:13

CHRISTMAS AND EASTER

'Twas the Night Before Christmas

SOMETIMES IT seems as if Christmas and all it pressures have become far too complicated, as this letter sent to me and written by a technical writer for a firm that does government contracting points out.

'Twas the nocturnal segment of the diurnal period preceding the annual Yuletide celebration, and throughout our place of resi-

dence, kinetic activity was not in evidence among the possessors of this potential, including that species of domestic rodent known as Mus musculus. *Hosiery was meticulously suspended from the forward edge of the wood burning caloric apparatus, pursuant to our anticipatory pleasure regarding an imminent visitation from an eccentric philanthropist among whose folkloric appellations is the honorific title of St Nicholas.*

The prepubescent siblings, comfortably ensconced in their respective accommodations of repose, were experiencing subconscious visual hallucinations of variegated fruit confections moving rhythmically through their cerebrums. My conjugal partner and I, attired in our nocturnal head coverings, were about to take slumberous advantage of the hibernal darkness when upon the avenaceous exterior portion of the grounds there ascended such a cacophony of dissonance that I felt compelled to arise with alacrity from my place of repose for the purpose of ascertaining the precise source thereof.

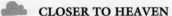

Hastening to the casement, I forthwith opened the barriers sealing this fenestration, noting thereupon that the lunar brilliance without, reflected as it was on the surface of a recent crystalline precipitation, might be said to rival that of the solar meridian itself – thus permitting my incredulous optical sensory organs to behold a miniature airborne runnered conveyance drawn by eight diminutive specimens of the genus Rangifer, *piloted by a minuscule, aged chauffeur so ebullient and nimble that it became instantly apparent to me that he was indeed our anticipated caller. With his ungulate motive power travelling at what may possibly have been more vertiginous velocity than patriotic alar predators, he vociferated loudly, expelled breath musically through contracted labia, and addressed each of the octet by his or her respective cognomen – 'Now Dasher, now Dancer …' et al. – guiding them to the uppermost exterior level of our abode, through which structure I could readily distinguish*

*the concatenations of each of the thirty-two
cloven pedal extremities.*

*As I retracted my cranium from its erst-
while location, and was performing a 180-
degree pivot, our distinguished visitant
achieved – with utmost celerity and via a
downward leap – entry by way of the smoke
passage. He was clad entirely in animal pelts
soiled by the ebony residue from oxidations of
carboniferous fuels which had accumulated
on the walls thereof. His resemblance to a
street vendor I attributed largely to the
plethora of assorted playthings which he bore
dorsally in a commodious cloth receptacle.*

*His orbs were scintillant with reflected
luminosity, while his submaxillary dermal
indentations gave every evidence of engaging
amiability. The capillaries of his malar
regions and nasal appurtenance were
engorged with blood which suffused the subcu-
taneous layers, the former approximating the
coloration of Albion's floral emblem, the
latter that of the Prunus avium, or sweet*

cherry. His amusing sub- and supralabials resembled nothing so much as a common loop knot, and their ambient hirsute facial adornment appeared like small, tabular and columnar crystals of frozen water.

Clenched firmly between his incisors was a smoking piece whose grey fumes, forming a tenuous ellipse about his occiput, were suggestive of a decorative seasonal circlet of holly. His visage was wider than it was high, and when he waxed audibly mirthful, his corpulent abdominal region undulated in the manner of impectinated fruit syrup in a hemispherical container. He was, in short, neither more nor less than un obese, jocund, multigenarian gnome, the optical perception of whom rendered me visibly frolicsome despite every effort to refrain from so being. By rapidly lowering and then elevating one eyelid and rotating his head slightly to one side, he indicated that trepidation on my part was groundless.

Without utterance and with dispatch, he

*commenced filling the aforementioned
appended hosiery with various of the aforementioned articles of merchandise extracted
from his aforementioned previously dorsally
transported cloth receptacle. Upon completion
of this task, he executed an abrupt about-face,
placed a single manual digit in lateral jux-
taposition to his olfactory organ, inclined his
cranium forward in a gesture of leave-
taking, and forthwith effected his egress by
renegotiating (in reverse) the smoke passage.
He then propelled himself in a short vector
onto his conveyance, directed a musical
expulsion of air through his contracted oral
sphincter to the antlered quadrupeds of
burden, and proceeded to soar aloft in a
movement hitherto observable chiefly among
the seed-bearing portions of a common weed.
But I overheard his parting exclamation,
audible immediately prior to his vehiculation
beyond the limits of visibility: 'Ecstatic
Yuletide to the planetary constituency, and to
that self-same assemblage, my sincerest wishes*

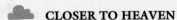

for a salubriously beneficial and gratifyingly pleasurable period between sunset and dawn.'

Phew! This year give me just an old-fashioned Christmas with family, friends and the new hope that a tiny baby brings to us all.

Bethlehem

A little child
A shining star.
A stable rude,
The door ajar.

Yet in that place,
So crude, forlorn,
The Hope of all
The world was born.

AUTHOR UNKNOWN

Good Friday

GOOD FRIDAY! Ever since I was a kid I wondered why today was called Good Friday. What's good about it? The finest man who ever lived nailed to a block of wood and over a period of six hours tortured to death. We do not know, we cannot tell what pain he had to bear but we've got a good idea. We've read about crucifixion, we know it was slow and agonising. The victim had to endure the pain of nails through his hands and feet, the burning Middle Eastern sun before, exhausted, the sheer weight of his own body hanging from the cross brought about asphyxiation. Bad enough for a common criminal but when you believe that it was the Son of God who hung there it's too awful to think about. So how could it possibly be called Good Friday?

Ernie Rae is a really good friend of mine. He's an ordained minister of the Presbyterian Church and was, for more than a decade, Head of Religious

Broadcasting at the BBC. He told me a story that helps to make some sense of Good Friday. As a theology student training for ordination, he volunteered to spend four months in a church in Winnipeg, Canada, where the congregation were what we used to call Red Indians, now they're Native Americans. These people had been displaced from their lands during the last century and now live in cities and towns, an environment completely alien to them. They suffer very high rates of unemployment, they are vulnerable to drink and the crime rates are very high. One of the most prominent church members was a man in his sixties called Bill. Bill was a craftsman; he carved things from wood and he shaped metal. One day they were talking together in Bill's home when Ernie's eye fell on a beautifully carved cross standing on the mantelpiece. He took it down to examine it, as you do, and realised that it was made from a knife. The base of it was the point, very sharp; it got broader as it went upwards and, at the top, the handle had been cleverly teased round to form the cross beam. Ernie asked Bill to tell him the story of the knife.

One night twenty years earlier, Bill's brother took his son out for a drink. One drink became two and soon they were roaring drunk. They exchanged cross words, then blows were struck. Bill's nephew pulled a knife and plunged it into his own father's heart, killing him instantly. At the trial the young man pleaded guilty to murder and was sentenced to twenty years' imprisonment.

You can imagine the impact on the family. They had been close-knit. This was no premeditated crime, it was the result of something that got completely out of control under the influence of drink. It left their lives shattered. Bill had his Christian faith to fall back on. He took the murder weapon home with him. For some years it lay in a drawer in his workshop. Several times he thought of throwing it away but couldn't bring himself to do it. One day he took it out, laid it on his workbench and began to polish and shape it into the form of a cross. It was the only way Bill could make sense of the tragedy. It was his belief that, on Good Friday, God so loved the world that he took all the evil and sin of that world upon his own shoulders; as the hymn says:

He died that we might be forgiven,
He died to make us good,
that we might go at last to heaven,
saved by His precious blood.

Bill transformed the dagger, the instrument of evil that had killed his brother and destroyed his family, into the symbol of God's love. It was his way of saying that he believed love was stronger than hate and good would triumph over evil. So that is why this is *Good* Friday because on this day, God used an instrument of torture to bring about our salvation.

Good Friday Prayer

MY SON RORY wrote this very moving Easter prayer:

I don't know how I knew it
For I wasn't there to see
But the tears He cried that afternoon
I know He cried for me.
P'raps I read it in the Bible
That, as on the cross He died,
For each one of my sins
A single tear He cried.
Not for my sins only
And not for me alone
But for each one of my fellow men
For their sins to atone.
Now He sits in judgment
As we kill and steal and maim
And cries because He knows
He needs to come and die again.

Easter Day!

AH, EASTER! What a great feast, in fact the greatest feast in the Christian calendar. Without the resurrection, everything is meaningless. We are, after all, 'The Easter People' and at Easter we proclaim our belief in the Risen Lord and cry out, 'He is risen, He is risen indeed!' I just love doing that, don't you?

One year I spent Easter in Cyprus, 'the Island of Saints', as it likes to be called. I was there to present *Good Morning Sunday* live from outside the Cathedral of St John in Nicosia on Easter Day. The thing that impressed me most while I was there was the Holy Week services. Churches were packed every evening culminating with Good Friday when, it seemed, the entire population of the capital was on the streets. The church we went to was packed to suffocation and there must have been 500 people outside the church, peering in through its open doors. The service was relayed to them by loud-speakers. After a while, those inside the church

91

began to file out through the two side doors and those outside formed themselves into a line to enter the church through the main door. Naturally, not wishing to miss anything, I joined the line as it shuffled forwards. I didn't know what to expect but thought that by the time I reached the front, I'd have a good idea of what was going on.

At the front of the church stood the *Epitaphis* beautifully decorated with flowers. This represents the bier upon which the body of the dead Christ was carried to the tomb. The line of people passed this on either side and, as they did, each took a flower petal from it. Behind the *Epitaphis* stood an empty cross. Each person knelt to kiss the cross, then exited the church via one of the side doors. Throughout this the priest – actually he was a bishop, Bishop Vassilius – was singing in Greek. I learned later that he was singing the Gospels relating to the arrest, condemnation and crucifixion of Christ. Once everyone had completed their veneration of the *Epitaphis* and the cross, four soldiers entered the church and, lifting the *Epitaphis* onto their shoulders, followed the bishop from the church in procession. The procession circumnavigated the church, then took off around the local streets with the majority of the faithful following.

How wonderful to see a nation in which religion and belief are still such an integral part of everyday life – where did we in the UK go wrong?

Confronted as I was by the empty cross in that church I was reminded of an eminent female theologian who told me she would never wear a crucifix. The empty cross, she said, was the only symbol for a Christian. It represents resurrection, the triumph over death. This bothered me. Had I got it wrong all these years? I went again to Birmingham Oratory to look at the crucifix that had so impressed me during my school days. Christ in torment. The muscles of the arms are taut as He hauls Himself up to relieve the cramp that threatens to crush His chest. I can hear the rending of flesh and the crunching of bone as He pulls on His hands and the life blood seeps out of Him along the wicked nails. As the crown of thorns bites cruelly into His head, agony and anguish contort His features so that no one seeing it can be in any doubt of the immense suffering He underwent for us. Yes, the empty cross promises me eternal life but only a crucifix can show me the price paid by my beloved Saviour for my salvation. Easter is not an empty cross, Easter is the broken body of Our Blessed Lord.

Easter People's Prayer

Dear God,
We are your Easter People.
There are so many different denominations
of Christians:
Roman Catholics, Anglicans, Baptists,
Methodists
as well as those who worship in the Orthodox
tradition.
We pray for the family of the Christian
Church
in which we are all brothers and sisters in
Jesus Christ.
Lord, keep us ever mindful of this
and help us to work together as the family we
should be.
We ask your Spirit of peace
on all areas of the world where there is
conflict
that at this time of resurrection,
new birth and hope,

*your Spirit of reconciliation will prevail
and the people of violence will be shown the
        folly of their ways.
Loving Father, we bless You for the joy of
        Easter Day
with its message of new life in Your Son
through the gateway we call death.
We thank you for the hope of eternity
and pray that we may live a Christ-like life
in the light of what is to come.
Finally on this day let us focus our minds
on the power of what was achieved on the cross
and on the joy of the resurrection.*

GOD'S CHARACTER

All Around

'FROM A DISTANCE' is a lovely song. However, whenever I play it on my programme, I receive a letter from the same lady listener telling me that the song is theologically incorrect.

'God is not watching us from a distance,' she says. 'God is all around us.'

I suppose in some ways she's right but I like to think that God watches us both from near and far at the same time!

She would, however, be in agreement with a little

97

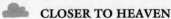

girl I heard about recently. Her Sunday school teacher was explaining where God was: 'As far as you can see to your left side, as far as you can see to the right, as far as you can see looking up and the same looking down, as far as you can see in front and as far as you can see behind, that is where God is. What have you got to say to that?'

She thought for a moment, then said, 'Aren't we lucky that we're right in the middle?'

I have found the Christ whose centre is everywhere and whose circumference is nowhere.

THOMAS MERTON

You're a Pea Hans

SKIING IS A passion I acquired in my mid-forties. I can't wait to go every year, I just love it. It's exhilarating, it's thrilling; I love the speed, I love the crisp, clear air. We go to a resort called Livigno, it's in Northern Italy and is truly beautiful. We fly into Bergamo, which is the birthplace of Pope John XXIII, but the majority of visitors to Livigno arrive by road. Europeans are great drivers and you'll find yourself sharing the slopes with Germans, Austrians and Swiss as well as Poles and Czechs. The French aren't much in evidence, they tend to stick to their own Alps. The last time they travelled extensively in Europe was during the Napoleonic wars.

I got onto a two-man lift one morning. A young chap joined me.

'Gud Morgan,' he said.

'Good morning,' I replied.

'Ach, you are English.'

'Yes,' I confirmed, 'and you are German.'

'No, no,' he said, 'I am from Holland.'

'Oh, Holland,' I said, 'I bet you're quite good at skiing with all those mountains.'

You know immediately when you've said the wrong thing, don't you? He looked at me strangely before averting his eyes. We spent the next five or six minutes in complete silence. Just as the lift reached the top, he turned to me, said, 'Holland is very flat', and skied off.

Europeans pride themselves that they understand English but they don't understand the English. A Frenchman was lecturing to a group of English salesmen at their annual sales conference.

We as a nation have been invaded many times, our culture has benefitted greatly from such invasions. You English, on the other hand, have been invaded only once in the last one thousand years. The Normans were sophisticated, they were wise, but did you English benefit from that? – No! That is what is wrong with the English, you never appreciated Norman Wisdom.

The entire audience collapsed in hysterics and the 'wise' Frenchman didn't have a clue why.

What a good job God is eloquent with every language in our crazy world!

Never Alone

WHEN I'M ALONE in my car I put a tape or a CD on and sing along at the top of my voice. I'm one of those boring people who can remember the words of most of the songs.

I was giving a lift to a friend one day. I just happened to have a tape by John Denver in the machine and as John began to struggle a bit on the high notes, I decided to help him out by duetting on 'Wild Montana Sky'. My passenger was appalled, the confined space and lack of an escape route adding to his discomfort.

'You don't 'arf sing loud,' he complained.

'When I'm on my own, I sing much louder than this,' I riposted.

'Blimey!' he exclaimed. 'I hope I'm never with you when you're on your own.'

This is one of the most encouraging of God's promises. That He will never leave us or forsake us. Right through the Bible from Moses to Joshua and into the New Testament, God repeatedly says, 'I will never leave you or forsake you.' Yet there is a certain amount of fear attached to this idea because we can sometimes imagine that God might be like an acquaintance who won't leave us alone, wanting to stalk us everywhere. But God isn't someone we are continually trying to shake off.

He will quietly be there at every moment of our day. He is not intrusive. He does not butt in. He does not shout out His opinions. He does not watch us with a judgmental eye. He does not try to control us. He is there because He loves us. He is interested in what we do and wants to be proud of us, like any good father.

He might even stay when I start to sing!

Technical Support

THIS IS ONE of my favourite e-mails, sent to me by someone who, like me, has experienced the panic of not being able to understand how their computer works. Who runs the technical support centre in heaven, do you think?

TECH SUPPORT: Yes Madam, how can I help you?

CUSTOMER: Well, after much consideration, I've decided to install Love. Can you guide me through the process?

TECH SUPPORT: Yes I can help you. Are you ready to proceed?

CUSTOMER: Well, I'm not very technical, but I think I'm ready. What do I do first?

TECH SUPPORT: The first step is to open your heart. Have you located your heart, Madam?

CUSTOMER: Yes, but there are several other programs running now. Is it OK to install Love while they are running?

TECH SUPPORT: What programs are running, Madam?

CUSTOMER: Let's see, I have past-hurt, low self-esteem, grudge and resentment running right now.

TECH SUPPORT: No problem, Love will gradually erase past-hurt from your current operating system. It may remain in your permanent memory but it will no longer disrupt other programs. Love will eventually override low self-esteem with a module of its own called high self-esteem. However, you have to completely turn off grudge and resentment. Those programs prevent Love from being properly installed. Can you turn those off, Madam?

CUSTOMER: I don't know how to turn them off. Can you tell me how?

TECH SUPPORT: With pleasure. Go to your start menu and invoke forgiveness. Do this as many times as necessary until grudge and forgiveness have been completely erased.

CUSTOMER: OK, done. Love has started installing itself. Is that normal?

TECH SUPPORT: Yes, but remember that you have only the base programme. You need to begin connecting to other hearts in order to get the upgrades.

CUSTOMER: Oops! I have an error message already. It says, 'error-programme not run on external components.' What should I do?

TECH SUPPORT: Don't worry, Madam. It means the Love program is set up to run on internal hearts but has not yet been run on your heart. In non-technical terms, it means you have to Love yourself before you can Love others.

CUSTOMER: So what should I do?

TECH SUPPORT: Can you pull down self-acceptance; then click on the following files: Forgive self; Realise your worth; Acknowledge your limitations.

CUSTOMER: OK, done.

TECH SUPPORT: Now copy them to the 'My Heart' directory. The system will overwrite any conflicting files and begin patching faulty programming. You also need to delete verbose self-criticism from all directories and empty your recycle bin to make sure it is completely gone and never comes back.

CUSTOMER: Got it. Hey! My Heart is filling up with new files. Smile is playing on my monitor and Peace and Contentment are copying themselves all over My Heart. Is this normal?

TECH SUPPORT: Sometimes. For others it takes a while, but eventually everything gets downloaded at the proper time. So Love is installed and running. One more thing before we hang-up. Love is Freeware. Be sure to give it and its various modules to everyone you meet. They will, in turn, share it with others and return some cool modules back to you.

CUSTOMER: I promise to do just that. By the way, what's your name?

TECH SUPPORT: Just call me the Divine Cardiologist, also known as the Great Physician, or just 'I AM'. Most people feel all they need is an annual check-

up to stay heart-healthy; but the manufacturer
(ME) suggests a daily maintenance schedule for
maximum Love efficiency. KEEP IN TOUCH!

God's Job

MARION SHARP from Northolt has been writing to me since I first started presenting *GMS*. She often comes up with little gems; this is one of them.

> *For his RE homework, an eight-year-old had to explain God. Not an easy task for any of us but it gave him no problem: 'One of God's main jobs is making people. He makes them to replace the ones that die so there will be enough to take care of things on Earth. He doesn't make grown-ups, just babies. I think that's because they're smaller and easier to make. That way He doesn't have to take up valuable time teaching them to walk and talk; He can leave that to mothers and fathers.*
>
> *'God's second most important job is listening to prayers. An awful lot of this goes on since some people like priests and things pray all the time, not just at bedtime. God doesn't have time to listen to the radio or watch TV because of this.*

'God sees everything and hears everything and is everywhere which keeps Him pretty busy so you shouldn't go wasting His time by going over your mom and dad's heads and asking Him for something they said you couldn't have.

Jesus is God's son. His Dad appreciates everything He's done, all the hard work on Earth so He's told Him that He doesn't have to go on the road anymore. He can stay in heaven. So now He helps His Dad out by listening to prayers and seeing things that are important for God to take care of. Sometimes He just takes care of them Himself without having to bother God.

You can pray anytime you want and they are sure to help you because they've got it worked out so that one of them is on duty all the time. You should always go to church on Sundays because it makes God happy and if there's anybody you want to keep on the right side of – it's God. He put me here and He can take me back anytime He pleases.'

Rugby Speaks Louder than Words

I'M AN EXPERT on rugby football, you know – I am! The day following an international I stay close to the phone in case Clive Woodward rings to ask my opinion on how individuals performed or if there are any new tactics I feel he should employ. During each World Cup match I had all the answers: 'Bring on Mike Catt at half-time, it'll take the pressure off Jonny' – he must have read my mind which is probably why he's not rung yet ... but he surely can't continue to coach the national side without my advice for much longer?

Rugby's a great game because it's for people of all shapes and sizes. Little stocky blokes with no necks become props while those with long arms and short legs become hookers. If you're 6 foot 5 with retractable ears, you'll be a second row and if you want the ball desperately and are prepared to chase all over the field in pursuit of it, you'll be a flanker. Height and weight are advantageous in the forwards but behind the pack, size doesn't matter as much as speed, flair and good hands. You'll often see a back catch a high ball then set off up field at pace but when the opposition close in on him, the cry will go up, 'Give it to the big man!' If he's sensible, he'll offload to a prop or a second row who can go into contact, take the hit, shield the ball, stand his ground.

God's there for us, like a tall, solid, second row forward. You can hold on to the problems of life if you want to, you can run full tilt into the front row of despair or you can ask for help. Look round for the big man, he'll be there, at your shoulder, waiting for the offload.

Do not be afraid, for I am with you.
ISAIAH 43:5

Satan's Menu

GOD POPULATED the Earth with broccoli and cauliflower and spinach so that the man could live a long and healthy life but Satan created fast food outlets and hamburger joints in abundance.

So God created red, yellow and green fruit of all kinds and Satan brought forth the double cheeseburger and said to the man, 'Do you want sour cream and relish with that?'

And the man said, 'Not 'arf, pile it on.'

Satan piled it on and the man piled on the pounds.

God cried out with a loud voice, 'Try my fresh salad', but Satan created ice-cream and the man gained more pounds.

And God said, 'I have sent thee heart-healthy vegetables and olive oil in which to cook them.'

But Satan created huge steaks and butter and lard and grease and the man's cholesterol went through the roof.

And God brought forth sports that would give

exercise in the open air but Satan created satellite television and Sky Sports 1, 2 and 3. And God brought forth running shoes with air-cushioned insoles and ankle support and the man said he would use them to exercise and shed those extra pounds but Satan created the remote control so the man would not even have to toil to change channels.

And God opened gyms and health clubs and the man paid his membership but never went.

And God brought forth the potato, a vegetable low in fat and brimming with nutrition, but Satan created potato crisps, tacos, nachos and dips in which to plunge them. And the man clutched his remote control and ate his crisps. Life was easy and it tasted good but the man went into cardiac arrest.

God sighed a big sigh and created quadruple heart-bypass surgery but Satan controlled the health service.

Checkmate!

There is a way that seems right to a man, but in the end it leads to death.

PROVERBS 14:12

Trying to Connect You

WHEN PEOPLE complain that theatre bookings are dropping off I can tell them why immediately. I've just this minute put, or rather slammed, the phone down having hung on for half an hour trying to book tickets for a concert at the NEC.

'If you require details of our concerts, press one. If you wish to make a booking, press two.'

So I press two.

'If you wish to make a group booking, twelve tickets or more, press one, for lesser numbers of tickets, press two.'

I press two.

'Please hold, one of our booking operatives will be with you shortly. Your conversation may be recorded for training purposes, if you have any objection to this please press hash now.'

By now I'm rapidly losing the will to live. I couldn't care less if they film me in 3D, I just want to speak to a human.

'I'm sorry, all our booking operatives are busy at

present, your call is in a queue and will be answered in order. You are currently number [robotic voice butts in] se-ven-te-ee-en. Please hold.'

Having very little holding capacity, I slammed the phone down.

It reminded me of this, which was sent to me by a listener in Truro, Joan Miller:

Hello and welcome to the Mental Health Hotline.

If you are an obsessive-compulsive, press one repeatedly.

If you are co-dependent, please ask someone to press two for you.

If you have multiple personalities, press three, four, five and six.

If you are paranoid, we know who you are and what you want. Stay on the line so that we can trace your call.

If you are delusional, stay on the line and your call will be transferred to the mother ship.

If you are schizophrenic, listen carefully and a

*small voice will tell you which number to
press.*

*If you are a manic-depressive, it doesn't matter
which number you press, no one will
answer.*

*If you have a nervous disorder, please fidget with
the star key until a representative comes on
the line.*

*If you have amnesia, press eight and state your
name, address, phone number, date of
birth, social security number and your
mother's maiden name.*

*If you have run out of medication prescribed to
help you relax, press hash.*

*If you have a bipolar disorder, please leave a
message after the beep or before the beep or
after the beep. Please wait for the beep.*

*If you have short-term memory loss press nine, if
you have short-term memory loss press nine,
if you have short-term memory loss press
nine.*

*If you have low self-esteem, please hang up, all
our operators are too busy to talk to you.*

Isn't it wonderful to know that even though you can't get through to these people, you can always talk to God at any time, day or night?

Hotel Bibles

I'M ON THE road quite a lot. Summer seasons, tours, cabaret all seem to be one-nighters these days so I'm driving as much as ever. *GMS* comes live on a Sunday morning from Manchester or London but at Christmastime it can come from Birmingham, Southampton, wherever I'm in panto.

Arriving in time for the gig, and coming out of the stage door after dark, I never get a decent look at the surroundings. I get my fair share of hotel rooms to stay in but they're very samey. I could be staying anywhere except home. It probably seems quite glamorous but, unless Toni's with me, it can sometimes be a pretty lonely business.

One day I picked up one of the Gideons' Bibles and found the following inscription, obviously written by some wag: 'With compliments from the Author.'

It just reminded me that wherever I go, God got there before me.

God's Positive Answers

FOR ALL THE negative things we have to say to ourselves, God has a positive answer.

You say: 'It's impossible.'

God says: 'What is impossible with men is possible with God.' (Luke 18:27)

You say: 'I'm too tired.'

God says: 'I will give you rest.' (Matthew 11:28–30)

You say: 'Nobody really loves me.'

God says: 'I love you.' (John 3:16; 13:34)

You say: 'I can't go on.'

God says: 'My grace is sufficient.' (2 Corinthians 12:9; Psalm 91:15)

You say: 'I can't figure things out.'

God says: 'I will direct your steps.' (Proverbs 3:5–6)

You say: 'I can't do it.'

God says: 'You can do all things.' (Philippians 4:13)

You say: 'I'm not able.'
God says: 'I am able.' (2 Corinthians 9:8)

You say: 'It's not worth it.'
God says: 'It will be worth it.' (Romans 8:28)

You say: 'I can't forgive myself.'
God says: *'I forgive you.'* (1 John 1:9; Romans 8:1)

You say: 'I can't manage.'
God says: 'I will supply all your needs.'
   (Philippians 4:19)

You say: 'I'm afraid.'
God says: 'I have not given you a spirit of fear.'
   (2 Timothy 1:7)

You say: 'I'm always worried and frustrated.'
God says: 'Cast all your cares on *me*.' (1 Peter 5:7)

You say: 'I don't have enough faith.'
God says: 'I've given everyone a measure of
   faith.' (Romans 12:3)

You say: 'I'm not smart enough.'
God says: 'I give you wisdom.' (1 Corinthians
   1:30)

CLOSER TO HEAVEN

You say: 'I feel all alone.'
God says: 'I will never leave you or forsake you.'
  (Hebrews 13:5)

Lead Us, Heavenly Father, Lead Us

I WAS WALKING down the road when a small dog turned the corner in front of me and walked towards me. He was on a lead but there was no sign of his owner. He'd actually passed me by the time his owner, holding onto the other end of the lead, hove into view. Of course, an extending dog lead, what a great invention. I began to get silly thoughts as I often do. Is there a button to retract the lead rapidly? Could you be walking towards a dog who suddenly shot backwards round the corner and out of sight because his owner had pressed a button? Could people living in high-rise flats lower their pooch from their balcony and, when walkies time was over, just press a button and up he'd come?

Then I thought, what if God had each of us on a lead which He could retract if we looked like straying from the straight and narrow. Imagine a chap standing in front of the jeweller's window, brick in hand, when suddenly – whoosh, he's over the far side of the road. Jerusalem pick-pocket, busy shopping centre, surrounded by people – whoosh, he's in the desert with only a palm tree for company, still there's plenty of opportunity for a date.

It'd make life easier wouldn't it? Make the receipt of our heavenly reward a certainty, but would we resent it? Freedom of choice is God's gift to us. He allows us to be as good or as wicked as we like.

God's Pitch

DAVID SNOWLING from Kesgrave near Ipswich is a football referee and also a *GMS* listener. At the start of the season, he sent me this wonderful analogy of life with God.

> *The Man in Black has to have the following items in his possession when he starts a game.*
>
> *First the notebook, this reminds us of our Bible which helps us to live our daily lives.*
>
> *Next two cards, reminding us of the New and Old Testaments. The yellow one tells you that you have been cautioned. Are we cautious when we speak about our relationship with God? The red one tells you that you're being sent off – we recall that God sent His Son to save the world.*
>
> *Then the stopwatch, this is frequently stopped and started during the game. Do we stop and start our relationship with our*

church or with God? Can we honestly say we give God the time we should?

The whistle, *some refs are said to be 'whistle happy'. Are we happy to blow on things that we know are not right for us?*

The coin, *this is spun to decide which team kicks off. I wonder how many of us, on a cold Sunday morning, do this to decide whether to come to church or stay in bed?*

As we walk onto the pitch, we're greeted by a crowd, *sometimes large, sometimes small, reminding us that Jesus said, 'Where two or three are gathered in My name, there am I also in their midst.'*

We check the four corner flags *and remember that there were four apostles, all upright men: Matthew, Mark, Luke and John.*

The goalposts *make us wonder, when did I last score for God?*

One last item: the football. Do I kick God about like one of these or am I like Beckham, keeping possession until the time is right to pass His love on to others? Don't let God be your substitute, make Him your star player and, with Him at your side, you'll never walk alone.

The final whistle blows, what's the score? When God blows the final whistle on our lives, what will the score be?

A Perfect Altar

I DO TRY TO follow Jesus but not when it comes to carpentry. Jesus was a carpenter – Tubby Clayton was a padre, an army chaplain. During the First World War, he took possession of a house in Poperinge, a few miles behind the British front-line trenches at Ypres, or Wipers if you prefer. His intention was to have a place where men who had been in battle, and would shortly again be, could relax from the horrors of war. Over the doorway he put his motto, 'Abandon rank all ye who enter here.'

The attic was long and thin and ran the full length of the house. Tubby decided to turn it into a chapel. 'I'll need an altar,' he said to the three tommies who'd volunteered to help him with his task. 'Go and find a reasonably large table, anything will do'.

'We've got something,' they announced when they returned. 'It's a bit bulky but it's all we could find.' They struggled to get it up the three flights of stairs and when they did, Tubby saw that it had several drawers in it and a vice attached to one end. Unknowingly, the tommies had brought, not a table, but a carpenter's workbench.

'Will it do for an altar?' they asked.

'It's perfect,' said Tubby, turning away to hide the moisture in his eyes.

Born Again

I REALLY LIKE those people who officially call themselves 'Born Again Christians'. I've never met a miserable one and they're always keen to share 'The Good News' with anyone they meet. Their overzealousness can, however, get up your nose a bit, as Joe Pasquale would say: 'I've got a friend who'll get on your nerves.'

Over the years I've received many a well-meaning letter from a BAC, telling me that I'll be going to hell because they assume that I've not been 'born again'. Here's an example:

> *It would be dreadful to think that you will miss going to paradise, believing in God as you do. It's worth making sure even now that you are bound for heaven. There is only one way into heaven and that is through Jesus Christ, the door. You must be born again.*

John 3:3 tells me that 'no-one can see the kingdom

of God unless he is born again', and I am quite keen on that. However, for me it's not the terminology that matters so much as the process that God takes us through in order to become a new creation in Him. It seems more important to make sure that I have accepted Christ as my Lord and Saviour, rather than worrying about what I should call myself.

I don't believe there is a 'them and us' situation as if there is a two-tiered system going on in the heavenlies. Perhaps we get confused and worried about what seems to be a technicality, as if one Christian has prayed the right prayer and the other hasn't, and we end up using the words 'born again' like some sort of heavenly password.

As far as I am concerned, I am born again, not because of what I do, say or how I worship, but simply because Christ said that if I believe in Him and accept Him into my heart I am automatically 'Born Again'. If it's good enough for Him then it's good enough for me.

FAITH

Are You Sitting Comfortably?

I HAVE TWO CHILDREN, both grown up and moved away from the family home. Between the two of them, they accumulated nineteen GCSEs, six A levels and a university degree, yet not one of those qualifications equipped either of those kids to change a toilet roll when it was finished.

Why is that? Every time it happened, I'd get furious. I'd call them both into the living room where I would have a toilet roll as a visual aid. The conversation would go like this:

'This is a toilet roll. As you take paper away from it, it diminishes. That means it gets smaller. When all the paper has gone, you'll know because you'll be left with a cardboard tube of a completely different colour. At this point, you take the tube, you go into the laundry room, you open the cupboard where there are two hundred brand-new toilet rolls, you take one and you put it into the loo!'

But did they learn the lesson? Did they heck as like! Did I learn the lesson? No! I still never check before I sit down.

How many times does God have to tell us before we learn the lesson? It's amazing but true that the Bible says 'Do not fear' in one way or another 366 times. That's one 'Don't worry' for every single day of the week and one extra for leap year.

Like the loo paper that always needs to be there, I need to be reminded not to worry every single day.

Use Your Muscles

I BELIEVE THAT faith is rather like a muscle. You exercise it over many years, and the more you exercise it the stronger it gets. Eventually it is strong enough to withstand any strain. Muscle that is developed quickly over a short period of time doesn't have that strength in depth and may well stretch and snap.

I have great admiration for people of faith like Billy Graham and Luis Palau. Not only do they have muscular faith, they also have great humility. Through them Jesus has made an impact on many an individual and they have given their life to God.

However, the people who really count are the mission back-up team who ensure that those people who have committed themselves to God so suddenly are helped at a local level to develop their new-found faith, to work out on the treadmill of belief and to build up that muscle I was talking about.

So, don't be tempted to go for a quick spiritual

fix. Learn to enjoy building up the strength of faith that many conventional Christians have been quietly working on for most of their lives.

> *A farmer went out to sow his seed ... Some fell on rocky places, where it did not have much soil. It sprang up quickly, because the soil was shallow. But when the sun came up, the plants were scorched, and they withered because they had no root.*
>
> MATTHEW 13:3–6

How to See God

Does your mind play tricks on you? Mine does. We often fear the worst even when we've nothing solid to base our worries on. So it is with God. We often see Him in a way that is totally different from how the Bible describes Him. This is because we base our idea of Him on what we have experienced of people around us and what our imagination dictates. Someone once said to me that 'God is never disillusioned with you, because He has no illusions about you in the first place!'

It's true, God knows me inside out and accepts me just as I am, but do I do the same for God? This mind-jogger was sent to remind me that God isn't all I imagine!

At first I saw God as my observer, my judge, keeping track of the things I did wrong, to know whether I merited heaven or hell when I die. He was out there, like the Prime Minister. I recognised His picture when I saw it, but I really didn't know Him.

Later on, when I met Christ, it seemed as though life was rather like a bike ride, but it was a tandem bike, and I noticed that Christ was on the back helping me pedal.

I don't know just when it was that He suggested we change places but life's not been the same since.

When I had control, I knew the way. It was rather boring but predictable ... It was the shortest distance between two points.

But when He took the lead, He knew delightful long cuts, up mountains, through rocky places at break-neck speeds. It was all I could do to hang on! Even though it looked like madness, He said, 'Pedal.'

I worried and was anxious and asked, 'Where are You taking me?'

He laughed and didn't answer and I started to learn to trust.

I forgot my boring life and entered the adventure. When I say, 'I'm scared', He leans back and touches my hand. He takes me to people who have gifts that I need; gifts of healing, acceptance and joy. They give me gifts to take on the journey, my Lord's and mine.

And we're off again. He says, 'Give the gifts away, they're extra baggage, too much weight.' So I do, to the people we meet, and I find that in giving I receive, yet still our burden is light.

At first I don't trust Him to be controlling my life. I think, 'He'll wreck it!' But He knows bike secrets, knows how to make it bend to take sharp corners, knows how to jump to clear high rocks, knows how to fly to shorten scary passages.

And I'm learning to shut up and pedal in the strangest places. I'm beginning to enjoy the view and the cool breeze on my face with my delightful constant companion, Jesus Christ.

And when I'm sure I just can't do anymore, He smiles and says … 'Pedal'.

The Bright Side

'HOW ARE YOU?' we say when we greet someone or perhaps, 'How are you doing?' Or 'You all right?' These are the most meaningless questions in the English language. Have you ever tried to answer such a question?

'Well, not too good really. I've got this terrible sore throat, the stomach ulcer's playing up again and the doctor says I may have to have my leg off.'

Ten to one, the other person, not having listened to a word you've said, will reply, 'That's nice, see you soon', which is another insincere phrase. It'll probably be years before you bump into him again.

Someone I knew was ever so ill. He didn't look too good either. The chemo had taken its toll but whenever he was asked, 'How are you?' he'd reply, 'Bloody marvellous' with great enthusiasm. He could have given his questioner details of weight loss, hair loss and the severe pain to which he was subjected but that wouldn't have done him or them any good so 'Bloody marvellous' was the response even when, not much later, he was confined to the hospice. I'm sure that when the good Lord said to him, 'Come in, my good and faithful servant', his response would once again have been 'Bloody marvellous!'

God knows exactly how we feel, and still loves us, but can we risk being more honest with one another?

Keep Calm

'Give me patience but give it to me now!'

I'VE GOT NO PATIENCE. I've tried but it just doesn't work for me. I shout at traffic lights, 'Change!' I stand in front of the microwave and shout, 'Hurry!' I blame my mother. She did everything at a hundred miles an hour. When I went to grammar school, at the age of eleven, I still had difficulty dressing myself because, if I was being slow, Mom would step in and do it for me. Before I knew what had happened, all my buttons would be done up, my shoelaces tied and we'd be out the house. She was greased lightning was Mom and, in an attempt to keep up, I became like her. So I can't stand slow people, people who faff about. They drive me mad.

Patience, though, is a virtue we're told, or is it? Ambrose Bierce tells us that 'Patience is in fact a minor form of despair disguised as a virtue'. I don't feel so bad now.

But what of Job? He had patience and he certain-

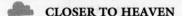

ly despaired. Did having patience do him any good?
Well yes, it was his God-given ability to be patient
that actually got him through his suffering.

Job probably asked God to take away his suffering but God said, 'No! Instead I'll give you the
patience, the strength, the resilience, in fact all that
you need to get through it.'

God never gives us a rucksack too heavy to carry.

What Prints?

One night I had a wondrous dream,
One set of footprints there were seen,
The footprints of my precious Lord.
But mine were not along the shore.
But then some stranger prints appeared,
And I asked the Lord, 'What have we here?'
Those prints are large and round and neat,
But, Lord, they are too big for feet.'
'My child,' He said, 'you are not wrong,
For miles I carried you along.
I challenged you to walk in faith,
But you refused and made me wait.
You disobeyed, refused to grow,
The walk of faith, you would not know,
So I got tired, I felt real glum,
And there I dropped you on your bum.
Because in life, there comes a time,
When one must fight, and one must climb.
When one must rise and take a stand
Or leave their bum prints in the sand.'

Shining Brightly

MIKE COYLE from Clevedon in Somerset reminds
me that it's important to pray …

> *Why do you light a candle, Ma,*
> *Like the one you lit today?*
> *The candle I lit today, love,*
> *Is to help me as I pray.*
> *When I kneel before the altar*
> *Or a picture of Our Lord*
> *I make my prayer in silence*
> *For I know it will be heard.*
> *And the candle which I've lighted*
> *With its soft and gentle glow*
> *Will light the way to heaven*
> *For my prayer from here below.*
> *Then as you seek some favour*
> *Or blessing from above*
> *Let the glow of your small candle*
> *Shine upwards with your love.*

CHILDREN AND FAMILIES

Our Fathers

'FATHER'S DAY – it's just an excuse for the greetings card companies to sell more cards.' You've heard that said, haven't you? Well, I think Father's Day is great. It gives my children the opportunity to reinforce a belief I've had for the past thirty-four years, that I am probably the finest father in Great Britain.

Last Father's Day, Jim Pritchard from Bude, Cornwall, decided to wax lyrical on behalf of us dads. He came up with this:

CLOSER TO HEAVEN

Why are dads so clever? There's nothing they can't do,
They mend your bike or roller skates, clean shoes to
*   look like new.*
They dig the garden, plant the flowers, grow
*   tomatoes by the score,*
They paint the house, pave the drive and mend the
*   garage door.*
They can make a kite or make a boat with rudder
*   and white sails*
When all they have to work with is wood and rag
*   and nails.*
They mend the car when it won't go, they don't
*   need a mechanic,*
The lights go off and, in a tick they're back, no time
*   to panic.*
They light the barbecue – no fuss then cook chicken
*   bits and steak*
Where did they learn to do such things and how
*   long did it take?*
Of course all dads are marvellous, I think I always
*   knew it*
Ah, but moms are even cleverer 'cos they tell dads
*   when to do it.*

Fathers' Prayer

We ask your blessings, Lord, on all fathers
that they will realise their responsibilities
that they will give their children
that most precious of all gifts
their time
and that they will always be worthy
of the love their children have for them.
We give thanks for our own fathers
for the love and support
  the wisdom and guidance we have received from
      them
  and we pray for those who are unable to give thanks
for those who never knew their father
and for those who for whatever reason
feel that their father has hurt them or let them
      down.
May they know your healing presence
And the love of their Father in heaven
that will never let them go.
Amen

Fishes and Men

THERE'S A LOT of fishing goes on in the Bible. Whenever I read a bit that mentions fish, I think of my dad. Dad was a fisherman; well, an angler actually. On a Sunday afternoon, he'd pack Mom and me into the car and we'd nip off to some stretch of water where Dad would spend the afternoon first impaling then drowning maggots. Sometimes the fish wouldn't take the hook, he'd just give the maggot a nasty suck. That really annoyed Dad. He'd reel in the line, remove what was left of the maggot, impale another and launch it into the middle of the river. I'd feel sorry for the once succulent maggot, lying flat and still on the bank. He'd now never achieve his ambition, never get his pilot's licence, never soar into the sky with the Bluebottle Airforce.

There are plenty of interesting places to fish; places where there are swings alongside the river, ice-cream vans, fields where you might meet other kids. We never went to them. Such places of excess population were to be avoided like the plague as far as Dad was concerned. He preferred to fish in places nobody else went to, in fact he fished in places nobody else knew about.

Not another living soul in sight, it was so quiet you could hear the snails breathing. Dad was in ecstasy, sat on his creel, eyes glued to the float bobbing up and down in front of him. If I spoke, the only response I'd get was, 'Ssssh, you'll frighten the fish.'

Yes, Mom and I spent many a silent Sunday on the riverbank. When I was about nine, Dad joined a fishing club. They had their own pool, which was reached by climbing a five-barred gate and traipsing through waist-high undergrowth. Not much chance of encountering other humans there, then. The pool was stocked annually; it was literally alive with fish. I've always thought that fish were far more intelligent than the blokes that try to catch them but this lot couldn't wait to get out of the water. They'd jump up and catch the hook while it was still in mid-air. Dad was in his element. In no time at all he'd have a keep-net full of dace, roach and perch, all of which he'd carefully replace in the pool before we left so that he could catch 'em again next week no doubt.

One Sunday, Dad couldn't wait for the afternoon. He set off for the pool before Mom and I left for nine o'clock mass. It had rained heavily overnight. Dad climbed the gate, arrived at the water's edge laden down with rods, creel and other accoutrements, slid down the muddy bank and ended up like Moses – in the bulrushes. Two anglers who'd heard the splash ran to his aid.

'How did you come to fall in?' they asked.

'I didn't come to fall in, I came to fish,' said Dad indignantly.

He carried on fishing, despite the fact that his boots and his underpants held several pints of water, and was rewarded. There was a big old pike living in that pool. A price was put on his head as he was busy eating up as many of the smaller fish as he could get down his neck. Dad hadn't set out to be a bounty hunter but just as he got his first bite of the day and began to reel in the tiddler, the rod was ripped from his grasp. The pike had taken the tiddler and the hook as well. Dad scrabbled for the rod and spent nearly an hour playing the big cannibal. The pike wrapped himself round the reeds as Dad brought him into the bank but Dad's trousers and footwear were already soaked so he went into the pool after him. He brought the fish home and placed it reverently on the kitchen table, he was so proud. Eventually, much to the relief of Mom and me, the pike went back to the fishing club, where it was no doubt stuffed and put in a display case, and Dad became a hero to the fishing club as well as to me.

Single Parents Find It Tough

WE'RE LIVING in an age when more and more children are being brought up by one parent, that parent is usually a mother. Many such ladies are doing a wonderful job but no matter how hard they try they can't be two parents, and a mom certainly can't be a dad. Moms provide the practical side of life; a mom is a cook, a laundress, a nurse.

If I'd had to bring up my kids on my own they'd have been unwashed and underfed but they'd have had fun.

Dads are fun. My dad worked long hours in a factory. He was tired and he slept a lot but he was interested in everything I did and went out of his way to support everything theatrical or sporting in which I was involved.

If I am a good dad, it's because I had him to show me how to be. If my son has children, he'll have learned how to be a dad from me but what of boys growing up now, who will be their template for fatherhood?

I don't think God intended kids to have just one parent but it's just a sign of how far from His intentions we've drifted.

Nevertheless single parents can be reassured that God is a loving heavenly Father who will help single parents have the strength and wisdom they need to be the best parents they can.

Daughters

I'VE GOT A GOOD friend named John. Of all the people I've ever met, he's got the sense of humour nearest to mine. When we're together we laugh continuously. John has a daughter who absolutely adores him, and why not? In the words of that advert, 'He's worth it!' At his sixtieth birthday, she insisted on making a speech; it was a short speech. She told the assembled gathering how important her dad was, how he'd always been there for her in her early life and during her difficult teens. She ended with the words: 'Anyone can be a father but it takes a real man to be a dad.' This was particularly poignant because, what I've not told you, John is not his daughter's biological father. She was born four years before John married her mother.

'You can have fun with a son but you've gotta be a father to a girl.' *Carousel* that comes from. Every man wants a son but every man should have a daughter. I'm particularly proud of my daughter, Rachel. She's a good mother, a loving wife, an outstanding Christian, she's very involved with the church and the children's liturgy. How much of this is down to me? I've often asked myself. When it was my sixtieth birthday, unknown to me, Rachel had been in touch with my producer, Rosemary. I was doing a link just before the programme finished when suddenly I heard Rachel's voice. She was on the phone to me.

'Hello, Dad,' she began. 'Are you surprised?'

Yes, I was. You could have knocked me down with a damp lettuce.

'It's your special birthday this week,' she continued. 'I've asked for this Celine Dion song to be played for you. The person who wrote it, wrote it for her father but the words could be about you and me.

As the record spun, so did my head and heart. You can imagine my feelings as the familiar song spoke about all the things that I had seen as important over many years of being a dad: always seeing the best in your child, being strong for them in their weakness, being their eyes, voice and ears above the world's noise, lending a hand just when they need

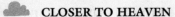

it, and above all showing them how important faith is.

When the song finished with the words 'For all the times you stood by me, for all the wrongs that you made right, I'm everything I am because you loved me', I was holding back the tears. It brought home to me in a very dramatic way that fathers have such a tough but vitally important job to do. As I took on board all the lovely things that Rachel had said about me through her choice of record, I was thankful that with God's help I seemed to have done OK.

From The Mouths
of Babes

LILY CARR WAS FROM Plumstead and apart from
being an extremely loyal GMS listener, she was also
a champion blood donor, having received their
highest award. She had no children of her own, but
loved stories about children. Whenever she heard
one, she'd pass it on to me.

> *At Sunday school, the children had been told*
> *about the importance of being good.*
> *'So what must we do to get to Heaven?'*
> *asked the teacher in conclusion. A hand shot*
> *up immediately.*
> *'Die' came the reply.*

> *A little girl was asked what she thought*
> *happened when people die.*
> *'Well,' she began, 'when we die we go up to*
> *Heaven then our feet come back and they*
> *grow another person and that's how we live*

157

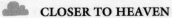

again.' It took ages to figure out where that had come from; the little girl had been told that the soul lives on. The only soul she knew was the sole of the foot – hence her theory of the afterlife.

The crib looked lovely as everyone went into mass on Christmas morning, but when they came out again, baby Jesus was missing. Who could have taken Him? The culprit was soon found. A young girl had the small statue in a brand-new pram which she was wheeling up and down outside church.

'What do you think you're doing?' asked her embarrassed mother.

'Well I prayed and prayed to Jesus for a pram for Christmas and I promised that if I got one, He could have the first ride.'

What Really Counts

ABOUT EIGHT YEARS ago, a national newspaper did a survey in which they asked primary schoolchildren what was the most important thing they could think of that would improve the world. Their answers were surprisingly similar.

'Everyone to be pleasant and like one another.'

'For all fighting and war to stop.'

'Enough food and clean water for all.'

'No more disasters like earthquakes and volcanic eruptions.'

But the one that caught everyone's eye came from a small boy who wrote: 'For all people to give your balls back when they land in their gardens.'

All the other kids spoke about things that they had no experience of. OK, they'd seen them on TV news programmes and documentaries, read about them in newspapers and magazines, but they were talking about something of which they had no direct knowledge while this young boy knew what would improve *his* life considerably.

Perhaps showing kindness and respect to our nearest neighbours will lead us into showing love and respect further afield. That's what really counts.

Keep Looking Up

IT WAS THE FEAST of St Joseph, the worker, a day of prayer for God's blessing on human work. The children's liturgy, conducted by my daughter, Rachel, was well under way. They'd talked about work and offering one's labours to God, then they talked about what they would be when they grew up.

'Pilot, nurse, teacher, explorer, dancer' – the ambitions were many and varied. My three-year-old granddaughter, Francesca, being the youngest was left till last.

'What do you want to be when you grow up, Cheska?'

'I want to be a rainbow,' came the reply.

The rain had just cleared up. It had been a downpour lasting nearly an hour but now they could get out. Raincoats were advisable but wellies were essential. The kids ran down the road, eager to splash in all the puddles. They came to a large, very oily puddle.

161

'Don't jump in that,' called out one kid earnestly.

'Why not?'

'Can't you see, there's a dead rainbow in it.'

Make sure you don't spend your time looking down in the puddles, when the real promise is up in the sky! Keep looking up!

Birds and Bees

I'VE JUST HAD a thought, Adam and Eve didn't have navels. Well, they couldn't have, could they? Unless the story Mom told me when I was small was true: 'Babies are made out of dough and baked in the oven. When they're taken out of the oven, God pokes them in the middle and says, "You're done."' Always sounded a bit unlikely to me.

I got a lot of enjoyment out of my belly-button. I used to play with it; any finger of right hand, insert into navel and rotate in clockwise direction. My mom used to get annoyed with me. She decided to frighten me out of it: 'All right, keep playing with your navel. Pretty soon you're gonna break it wide open, all the air will flow out of your body, you'll fly backwards round the room until all the air is gone then you'll lie there on the floor, flat as a piece of paper, just your little eyes sticking out – keep it up.'

She frightened me to death. It didn't stop me playing with my navel but, from then on, I always carried an Elastoplast in case I had an accident. Did you ever play volcanoes in the bath? What you do is lie in the bath having made sure that your tummy is completely dry. You then fill your navel with talcum powder and cough. Do write and let me know if you achieve a Vesuvian result.

A little girl had been told by her mother not to play with her navel. 'If you do that your tummy will swell and swell until you can hardly walk,' she'd said. The following day the mom took the little girl into Birmingham by bus. As the bus stopped at the next bus stop, an extremely pregnant woman called to the driver, 'Please wait.' Perspiring freely, she staggered onto the bus and collapsed into a seat opposite the little girl who stared unashamedly at the large lump. The mom-to-be was somewhat disconcerted by this overt attention; she leaned towards the little girl.

'Do you know me?' she asked.

'No,' replied the little girl, 'but I know exactly what you've been doing.'

BIBLE

The Earth Project

CONSERVATION STARTED in Birmingham, you know
– it did! In certain parts of Birmingham we've had
lead-free churches for thirty-five years to my knowledge!

If I'm honest I should have to concede that
greenism, as it's now called, started a long time
before that.

Having sat around for eons, doing various little
projects in various parts of the universe, God
decided to create the Earth. The Green Party of the
heavenly host immediately issued a summons for
Him to appear before them for failure to file an

environmental impact statement. At the hearing, God was asked: 'Why did you decide on this Earth project?'

'I was feeling a bit creative,' replied God.

'Oh yes, and what do you intend to do next?' asked the green angels.

'I thought I'd create light.'

'How will you do that?'

'I'll just say "Let there be light" and this huge ball of fire ...'

'Hold it right there,' said the chair angel. 'Ball of fire! What about all the smoke – pollution, can't have that!'

So God agreed to make light without any smoke and, in order to conserve energy, He'd only have light half the time. 'I'll call the light "day" and the darkness "night",' He said.

'But why have light at all? What do you want it for?' they asked.

'It'll make flowers and vegetables grow in abundance.'

At this point the Chief Agricultural Angel stepped in. 'As long as you realise that you must give an undertaking to avoid the use of pesticides, there'll be no genetic modifications, no foreign seeds, everything organic.'

'OK by me,' said God. 'Let the waters bring forth life and let fowl fly over the Earth …'

'Hang on!' said the angels. 'You can't just do that. We'll need the consent of the Angelic Fisheries Department and the Heavenly Wildlife Protection Federation.'

God started to get angry. 'I need to complete the whole thing in six days,' He ranted.

'No chance, pal,' said the spokesangel. 'It'll take two hundred days to review the application and the environmental impact statement. After that there will have to be a public hearing and even then it'll be twelve months before we complete the paper-work and you can begin.'

At that point, God created hell!

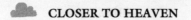

Psalm Twenty-three
-and-a-half

LISTENER PHYLLIS FRANKISH from Pontefract recently sent me this modern working of the twenty-third psalm:

The Lord is my pacesetter, I shall not rush
He makes me stop for quiet intervals.
He provides me with images of stillness which
    restore my serenity.
He leads me in ways of efficiency through
    calmness of mind
And His guidance is peace.
Even though I have a great many things to
    accomplish each day
I will not fret for His presence is here.
His timelessness, His all importance will keep me
    in balance.
He prepares refreshment and renewal in the
    midst of my activity

BIBLE

By anointing my mind with the oils of
*   tranquillity.*
My cup of joyous energy overflows.
Truly harmony and effectiveness shall be the
*   fruits of my hours*
For I shall walk at the pace of my Lord
And dwell in His house for ever.

Instructions Included

I'M NOT VERY GOOD with my hands. The first year at St Philip's Grammar School we had a double period of woodwork each week. I was bottom of the class by a long way. I made a cricket bat that no one could lift, a crucifix that leaned sideways at an angle of thirty degrees and a tray – ah, the tray! The Sunday after I took it home, Mom decided to use it for the first time. She was halfway up the stairs carrying three cups of tea when the bottom fell out of it. On my report, the teacher wrote, 'The only thing he's made successfully is sawdust.'

I now have friends and neighbours who are practical. In their garages they have chisels, pliers, hammers, electric drills, all neatly racked. I have no tools whatsoever. Since we got married I've never made anything, which is why I was curious when my wife took me to MFI.

'That looks nice,' she said. I had to admit that it did, one of the smartest wardrobes I'd ever seen and surprisingly cheap.

'We deliver anywhere in the country,' said the man obligingly.

'Must have a big lorry to get that in,' I thought – couldn't have been more wrong. A van drew up and out came two flat packs. Sellotaped to the one was a plastic bag containing screws, hinges and handles. I couldn't back down now. I borrowed tools from my near neighbours and set to assembly. The instructions in the flat pack were in Korean as well as English but I decided to abandon them and go it alone. I made a few adjustments with chisel, saw and lump hammer and I ended up with a bedroom shed. You wouldn't have had it in your house and it didn't stay in mine for long.

It always amazes me how people try and live without reading the Maker's instructions for life. God's little instruction book, the Bible, is jammed with all you need to know. Perhaps we should refer back to it more often.

Lessons from Noah

EVERYTHING I NEED to know, I learned from Noah's ark:

1 Don't miss the boat.
2 Plan ahead. It wasn't raining when Noah built the ark.
3 Stay fit. When you're 600 years old, someone may ask you to do something really big.
4 Don't listen to critics; just get on with the job that needs to be done.
5 Build your future on high ground.
6 For safety's sake, travel in pairs.
7 Speed isn't always an advantage. The snails were on board with the cheetahs.
8 When you're stressed, float awhile.
9 Remember, the ark was built by amateurs; the *Titanic* by professionals.
10 No matter the storm, when you are with God, there's always a rainbow waiting.

The Lost Chapter of Genesis

A DELIGHTFUL, very spiky female author by the name of Isobel Losada has been a guest on *GMS* more than once. She wrote a best-selling book called *The Battersea Park Road to Enlightenment* in which she investigated, at first hand, new age beliefs. It was a one-woman voyage through astrology, re-incarnation, anger management, tantric sex and inner goddesses. I must confess that I think she's delightfully barmy but they were great interviews and prompted heavy postbags. Isobel is very much a feminist, 'Anything a bloke can do, I can do better', so I decided to send her this …

Adam was hanging around the garden of Eden feeling very lonely so God asked him, 'What's wrong with you?' Adam said he was fed up 'cos he didn't have anyone to talk to. God said that He was going to make Adam a companion and it would be a woman.

'What's a woman, Lord?' Adam asked.

'A pretty creature who will gather food for you, cook for you and, when you discover clothing, she'll wash it for you. She'll always agree with every decision you make, won't nag you and will always be the first to admit she's wrong when you've had a disagreement. She'll bear your children and never ask you to get up in the middle of the night to take care of them. She will *never* have a headache and will freely give you love and passion whenever you need it.'

'Ah, come on, God, what would a woman like that cost?' asked Adam.

'An arm and a leg,' God replied.

Adam thought for a while, then asked, 'What can I get for a rib?'

The rest is history.

I should have expected it! A few days later back came the reply from Isobel ...

One day in the Garden of Eden, Eve calls out,
'Lord, I have a problem.'
    'What is it Eve?'

'Lord, I know you created me and provided this beautiful garden and all these wonderful animals, especially that hilarious comedy snake, but I'm just not happy.'

'Why not, Eve?' came the question from above.

'I'm lonely and I'm sick of apples.'

'Then Eve, I have the solution, I shall create a man for you.'

'What's a man, Lord?'

'A flawed creature with many bad traits who'll give you a hard time but he'll be bigger and faster than you and he'll like to hunt and kill things. Tell you what, since you've been complaining, I'll create him in such a way that he'll satisfy your physical needs. He'll revel in childish things like fighting and kicking a ball about. He won't be as smart as you so he'll need your advice to think properly.'

'Sounds great,' says Eve with an ironically raised eyebrow, 'but what's the catch? There must be a catch, Lord.'

'There is. You can have him on one condition.'

'What's that, Lord?'

'Well, as I told you, he'll be proud, arrogant and self-admiring so you'll have to let him believe that I made him first. It'll be our little secret – you know – woman to woman.'

Interviews I Wish I'd Done No. 1

MY GUEST THIS morning is truly remarkable. At an age when most people are busy deciding which retirement home they'd prefer to be in, this man has decided to change his name and, what's more, found a nation. It's Jacob, or should I say 'Israel' – good morning!

JAKE: I still answer to both names. The wife, Rachel, can't get used to it, still calls me Jake.

DON: As my dad always said, 'They can call me what they like as long as they don't call me too late for my dinner.'

JAKE: I had a brother like that. He'd give his birthright for a bowl of soup.

DON: Tell me, is there any precedent for this name-changing lark?

JAKE: Well, Muhammed Ali changed his name from Cassius Clay, Cliff Richard started life as Harry Webb and Prince changed his name to 'The Artist Formerly Known as Prince', which struck me as a bit stupid really.

DON: Well, yes, rather like Meatloaf changing his name to 'The Artist Formerly Known as Mince.'

JAKE: In fairness, it wasn't my idea.

DON: No?

JAKE: No! Me and God was having this wrestle, as you do, and God said, 'I want to name a nation and a land after you so you'll have to change your name.' I suggested Milcan, as in 'The Land of Milcan Honey' but he said it had to be Israel so He could call the people 'Israelites'.

DON: What's wrong with calling 'em 'Jacobites'?

JAKE: Too Scottish, He said.

DON: You don't think God's having you on, do you? After all, you're a bit of a practical joker yourself.

JAKE: How d'you mean?

DON: Well, you conned your dad out of giving you the blessing meant for Esau, you conned Laban out of his flocks by painting black stripes on 'em.

JAKE: Yeah, but look what Laban did to me. Seven years I worked so I could marry the beautiful Rachel and he conned me into marrying her sister, Leah.

DON: So?

JAKE: I was expecting a sex kitten, I got a bowwow.

DON: But you married Rachel in the end.

JAKE: Yeah, after seven years of Leah.

DON: She couldn't have been that bad.

JAKE: Well, no. Once I got used to the rugby team picking her in the front row instead of me, and her constant moaning about the moustache.

DON: You haven't got a moustache.

JAKE: No, but she has.

DON: So how has the rugby team done this season?

JAKE: We beat the Shechemites in the Covenant Cup.

DON: You didn't beat 'em. They never turned up, they were all lying around in agony at the time.

JAKE: Ah, yes, well, I was against that. I tried to warn 'em, give 'em a tip-off.

DON: They all had a tip-off from what I understand.

JAKE: It was my daughter, Dinah, who made the initial complaint.

DON: What exactly happened?

JAKE: Dinah was going out with this nice lad named Rodney but she met Prince Shechem at Dorcas's disco and he did the hokey cokey with her.

DON: The hokey cokey?

JAKE: In out, in out, Shechem all about. The whole thing left Dinah and Rod a bit drained.

DON: What's the situation with Dinah and Rod now?

JAKE: Dinah, Rod, they'll pull through.

DON: Well, Jacob – sorry, Israel – once the state's established perhaps you can come in again to tell us why Israel's always in such a state. Thanks for being with us on *GMS*.

Interviews I Wish I'd Done No. 2

DON: My guest this morning has taken the nation by storm. When it comes to single combat, he's the governor. The bigger they are the harder they fall and that's certainly true of anyone who dares to face David – good morning.

DAVE: Morning, good to be here.

DON: Well, yes. Yesterday few people would have given you much chance of being alive today, let alone appearing on Radio 2.

DAVE: Well, at the end of the day …

DON: At the end of the day what?

DAVE: At the end of the day I'm still here.

DON: What did you think when you first saw your opponent?

DAVE: I thought, my word you wouldn't get many of them in a dozen.

DON: Did you approach him with apprehension?

DAVE: No, just with a sling and a few pebbles.

DON: Ah, the pebbles. Who selects those for you?

DAVE: That'd be me dad, Jesse. He's tough. You have to be tough to live round here with a name like Jesse. If he finds a good pebble he gives it to my manager, Samuel or Sam the Man as he's known, and he puts a big tick on it.

DON: So that you'll recognise it?

DAVE: No, so that he can get me sponsored by Nike.

DON: So David, are you looking forward to a career in sport?

DAVE: Certainly not. It's so uncertain, one injury and it's all over. No, I'm doing an album, it's gonna be called *I Write the Songs*.

DON: Good title. And are you writing the songs?

DAVE: Yeah. I've wrote three up to now; 'Psalm enchanted evening', 'Psalm where over the rainbow' and 'We're all going on a psalmer holiday.'

DON: Fascinating!

DAVE: Then I'm doing a film for Spielberg, a nice Jewish lad, that's called *Lyre, lyre*.

DON: I'd have thought they'd want to make a film about your defeat of Goliath.

DAVE: Well, yeah, they're doing that as a biopic.

DON: Will you play yourself?

DAVE: No. They're getting Sylvester Stallone to play me.

DON: Well, that won't work. The whole point is that you're such a little feller.

DAVE: If you think I'm gonna let Danny de Vito dress up as me, you're out of your mind.

DON: Who's got the part of Goliath?

DAVE: There's no one big enough so he'll be computer-generated but the Philistines will be there for all the crowd scenes.

DON: And what's after that? More films, more recording?

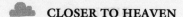

DAVE: No. Sam the Man says he's gonna get me a job as king after that.

DON: King! But there's already a king.

DAVE: Oh you mean Loony Toons?

DON: Loony Toons?

DAVE: Yeah. 'That Saul folks!' Speaking of which, must dash, I'll be late for the anointing.

DON: Well, p'raps we can invite you onto the show again once you've become king. Meantime, thanks for being with us on *Good Morning Sunday*.

Can God Really Use Me?

THE NEXT TIME you feel like God can't use you, remember the following people:

Noah *was a drunk* …
Abraham *was too old* …
Isaac *was a daydreamer* …
Jacob *was a liar* …
Leah *was ugly* …
Joseph *was abused* …
Moses *couldn't talk* …
Gideon *was afraid* …
Sampson *had long hair, and was a womaniser!*
Rahab *was a prostitute* …
Jeremiah *and* Timothy *were too young* …
David *had an affair and was a murderer* …
Elijah *was suicidal* …
Isaiah *preached naked* …
Jonah *ran from God* …
Naomi *was a widow* …
Job *went bankrupt* …

John the Baptist *ate bugs* …
Peter *denied Christ* …
The disciples *fell asleep while praying* …
Martha *worried about everything* …
Mary Magdalene *was demon-possessed* …
The Samaritan woman *was divorced* … *more than once!*
Zaccheus *was too small* …
Paul *was too religious* …
Timothy *had an ulcer* …
and Lazarus was dead!

Bible Hit Parade

HI THERE, POP PICKERS! It's me, Gabriel, homing in on a wing and a prayer to bring you this week's *Top Thirty*.

Coming in at No. 30, it's the Five Wise Virgins with 'Girls Just Wanna Have Fun'.

Down two places at 29, the man you love to hate – Judas Iscariot, 'It Started With a Kiss'.

And at 28: 'The Second Time Around', from Lazarus.

'It's Only Make Believe' by Doubting Thomas stays where it is.

But moving nicely – 'The Lady Is a Tramp' from Jezebel – don't dispute it, pop-pickers!

Galloping along as you'd expect, the Three Wise Men with 'There's Something 'Bout You Baby I Like'.

It's been there a while but slipping down fast to this week's No. 24, 'Raindrops Keep Falling On My Head' – Noah.

Straight in this week, at No. 23, the big new instrumental from Elijah – 'Chariots of Fire'.

Then comes our child prodigy, Jairus's Daughter – 'Wake Me Up Before You Go Go'.

No. 21's 'Gone Fishing' from Jonah.

And at 20, that huge disco hit, 'Dance Yourself Dizzy' by Salome.

That draws a veil over the bottom ten, now for the Top Twenty.

And this week's highest new entry: 'The Tide is High' – Pharaoh.

At 19, 'Walk On By' – The Priest, the Levite but not the Good Samaritan.

He's been twenty years in the chart but he's slipping down fast, the Old Lawgiver himself, Moses singing, 'The Wanderer'.

'I Believe in Miracles' by the Guests from the Marriage Feast at Cana stays at 17 for the second week running.

But down three places goes Daniel's 'The Lion Sleeps Tonight'.

At 15 and I don't think it's gonna make the Top Ten: 'I Feel The Earth Move Under My Feet' by the Massed Choirs of Sodom and Gomorrah.

No. 14, what a group they are! Paul and the

Corinthians: 'I'm Gonna Sit Right Down and Write Myself a Letter'.

Unlucky for some but not for this guy, the No. 13: 'I'll Never Find Another Ewe' – the Good Shepherd.

Hovering at the gateway to the Top Ten, will they make it next week? At 12 – Jeremiah: 'Take This Job and Shove It'.

And at 11, the Mount Tabor Singers: 'Up, Up and Away'.

Now it's Top Ten time – 'The Final Countdown' – and it is. At No 10: 'Final Countdown' - The Four Horsemen of the Apocalypse.

No. 9 is 'Stayin' Alive' from Methuselah.

No. 8: 'Message in a Bottle' – Jeroboam.

At 7: 'Don't Sit Under The Apple Tree With Anyone Else But Me' from Eve.

And at 6 – isn't this a coincidence – 'If You Were the Only Girl in the World' from Adam. Both these tracks taken from their great new CD, 'Strangers in Paradise'.

No. 5: 'Bob the Builder, Can You Fix It?' asks Joshua.

And at No. 4, another question: 'What's New, Pussycat?' – Samson and the Lion.

Now for the Top Three: at No. 3 and still climbing, 'We Will Rock You'– The Jerusalem Mob with the Woman Taken in Adultery.

We said it couldn't be done but do it they have, following their last two chart-toppers: 'Something's Burning' and 'The Heat Is On', the Red Hot Trio have done it again: 'C'mon, Baby, Light My Fire' by Shadrack, Meshach and Abednigo is this week's No. 2.

But still there at No. 1, topping for the third millennium running, God with 'Who can I turn to?'

The Bible in Fifty Words

God made
Adam bit
Noah arked
Abraham split
Joseph ruled
Jacob fooled
Bush talked
Moses balked
Pharaoh plagued
People walked
Sea divided
Tablets guided
Promise landed
Saul freaked
David peeked
Prophets warned
Jesus born
God walked
Love talked
Anger crucified
Hope died

CLOSER TO HEAVEN

Love rose
Spirit flamed
Word spread
God remained.